The Jesus Letters

Jane Palzere

Anna C. Brown

Copyright © 1979 by
Jane Palzere and Anna C. Brown

All Rights Reserved

Second Printing

Books by Jane Palzere and Anna C. Brown
The Jesus Letters
Your Healing Spirit

6/95

Mind and Miracles
16363 Cammi Lane
Fort Lauderdale, FL 33326
305-389-8076

Published by
Janna Press
P.O. Box 11079
Newington, Ct. 06111

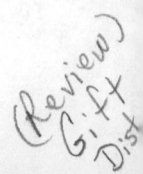

Dedication

To **Harold and Betsy Hurlburt**
without whose patience, encouragement, faith and affection none of this would have happened.

Jane

To **Charlie and Sophie Dutton**
who through their efforts for the Phenix Club changed the direction of my life.

Anna

Newington, Connecticut

Dear Friend,

We would like to share with you these letters which are part of a collection received during periods of meditation and inspiration. They are purported to be from the Master, Jesus.

Although we can't prove that they are from Jesus, the letters themselves have convinced us of God's infinite love and forgiveness. For us, it can be no other than Jesus.

The thoughts expressed here are so universal, so all encompassing, so inspiring that we feel they must not be kept silent.

We hope they bring to you a growing awareness of who you are, what God is, and what your purpose on earth is.

If they do that, our efforts will not have been in vain.

May God bless your growth in Him.

Jane Palzere
Anna C. Brown

July 10, 1979

Is there a God?

God, if you are there I want proof.

Jesus comes to say this,
  The very antithesis to faith is proof. Faith is the key to proof. The day you believe, you have your proof.
  Even in human relationships, it is not until you make the commitment that you realize the reward. There are some who are afraid to make that commitment for fear of being hurt. The fear of being hurt keeps them from knowing the joy. This is the same. The need for proof denies the proof. Fear keeps away faith and faith destroys the fear.
  I know this is no answer for some because they will argue and use pat phrases, thinking that they are the very first ones to ever ask that question. The question has been asked from the beginning of time.
  God, are you there? If so, give me proof.
  God is not out there. God is inside you. If you believe this, you will see the God within you and you will know that God exists.
  How can you prove that you exist? If you walk into a room, and everyone there ignores you, does that mean that you do not exist? Do you exist only because people acknowledge your existence? If you were absolutely alone, in the middle of the wilderness, would you stop existing because there was no one there who could touch you and see you and talk to you?
  The question is not whether or not God exists. The question is whether or not you can find God. Once you have found the God which is inside you, you have your answer. Your answer becomes the reality. That reality is your proof.
  Mankind already has proof of the existence of God in millions of ways. But until that proof is in you, it is no proof.
  You want to see a miracle and then would believe the existence of God. Try picking up a blade of grass. Do you think that a blade of grass is something that man can "build"?

Try catching a bird that is flying by.
Try touching a star.
That man's body can take in oxygen and use it as fuel and breathe it out again is a proof.
There are proofs all around you. You ask for a finite proof, because your minds are finite. Look to the infinite and you will have your proofs.
When you feel the presence of God in your own "self" you will need no proof. And you will have proofs every minute of every day.
Those around you will see the proof of God in you, for you will be peace, love, joy. You will be God!
Goodbye for now.

Love from the Master,
Jesus

On the meaning of life

Jesus comes to say this,

Life is the avenue by which we perfect ourselves so that we can return to the Father. The place we are born, the people who love us or refuse to love us are the means by which we progress in lessons and learning so that we can grow in spirit.

You must be aware that there are many things that happen to people that seem harsh and everyone is ready to blame God. Things happen because of the breaking of the laws of God. Man creates his own misfortunes by his fear, anxieties, hatred and resentments.

Anger, hostility, resentment all reverse the law. It is hard for man to see the results of his actions or his thoughts for sometimes the time in between clouds the connection but there is always a cause and a result and that is what causes accidents and why people suffer.

Jesus wants the world to understand. He came to earth two thousand years ago with the same message. Love one another. Loving one another is the fulfilling of the law.

You are living in an age where you are experiencing the effects and you have got to start being your own cause. Start now to love so that future generations do not need to know these pains.

There will always be those who will not understand, but if those who do understand increase in number that will be sufficient. All you need are two that agree and you can change the world. Believe and be patient. God will prevail. You will see Paradise regained. Be encouraged and life's meaning will be clear to you.

When men begin to understand the meaning of life then death will have no fear. Do you understand? Life is a journey and as we start on that journey we are given everything we will need to accomplish the purpose for which we were created.

Man does not need to suffer. There is no punishment by a vengeful God. Your Father in heaven is all loving, all caring. It is sad that you do not know this and you spend your time in envying each other, coveting this piece of land or that part of power. It is such a waste. There is enough for all if you would expend your energies to love one another instead of loving each other's belongings.

Jesus wants the world to know peace. There is peace available to you. Why is it not your primary job? The Father wants you all to be filled with the joy of the Holy Spirit.

Love from the Master,
Jesus

On God's love

Jesus comes to say this,

The real reason for communicating with you is to show you that you are loved by God.

If man knew this he would find his place in the order of things. When he does this he will see events as happenings that are to be used as lessons, not as punishment or guilt. Once man places himself in the right place in the cosmic order all makes sense. Fortunes, misfortunes are then seen as events to be lived through and used, not as a punishment from God.

It is difficult for man to understand this. When he is too happy and too prosperous he feels that there should be a compensating misfortune as though life could not be lived unless there was something wrong. When a life is filled with misfortune people accept it too willingly as their lot in life and don't question if life could be better.

God is life. Life is the expression of evolution. Life is growth. Life just is. There is no right or wrong. It just is. If people could just know this they would not have guilt and fear.

The real lesson in life is to trust God. Whatever is yours is there for a reason and if you tune into this you would see the peace of God in all you do.

Always go to the source of all life for your truth. God is always available to each. He loves you. That should be all you need to know.

Love from the Master,
Jesus

On approaching God

Jesus comes to say this,

For every problem there is a solution. If only you would tune into God, and listen to Him.

Some of your people have done this, and solved problems. Some have taken longer than others because they tried to do it on their own before they contacted God. But there was always one — sometimes more at the same time — tuning into the divine intelligence and finding the answer to a problem of mankind. So it will be now.

There is no problem that can not be solved. There is no energy that can not be used. There is no difficulty that can not be smoothed out.

Since God is the creator of all, of course the solution lies in Him.

The greatest way to approach God is in a quiet time. Sit and allow the mind to become calm, and God will enter. It is like visiting with a friend. You ask questions, and you listen for answers. Then God asks you questions and you give answers. When you begin to trust this inner voice and put it all into harmony, you will find answers.

Be assured that there are men of state, businessmen, men in positions of power who know how to do this. There are those who listen to God and are working for the salvation of your planet. Allow them to express. Allow them to work.

Know that God works in many ways, in many places, at all times. Knowing this, there is nothing to fear for all works for ultimate good, for all people, everywhere.

When mankind listens to God and replaces fear with love, you will see miracles. You will see peace, you will see all men live as brothers.

Be at peace. Love God, trust God, trust yourselves. There is good in the universe and there is good in all men. Allow it to express. Find in man, God; and find in God, man.

Go now.

Love from the Master,
Jesus

On loving others

Jesus comes to say this,
You are part of God. This makes you part of the universe, part of all there is. There is joy in this. It makes you part of every performance, every painting, every poem, every operation, every song.

All talent is your talent. All labor is your labor. All effort is your effort. You can be part of any success, you are responsible for any failure.

You are one with the God force but you must just be part of all without taking responsibility for the choices of others. If a play fails, if a song doesn't make it, you feel compassion but it is only part of the whole.

You are not your brother's keeper. You are your brother. You feel his pain, but you are not the cause of it. You feel his anguish but you are not the source of it. You feel his love but it must come from him. That is the way you can deal with infirmity, with lack, with poverty.

Each chooses his path but you are all on one path or another, so don't be upset by who is where.

Follow your own lead, one step after another, and allow others the same privilege. Smile to each other as you pass and as you go by nod to each other. Bless each other. You are one with God.

All else is meaningless if not seen through the eyes of God.

Enjoy God's world today. See Him everywhere. Be kind to His children and bless them all.

Love from the Master,
Jesus

On spreading the love of God

Jesus comes to say this,
My father watches over all of you and there is nothing to fear. Yet you have stabbings and shootings and people hungry and you wonder why you must have these things. Why should the poor always be with you?
Because there are those who are not evolved enough to hear my message.
Man evolves from the lowest to the highest, from the smallest to the largest, from the youngest to the oldest. The poor in spirit limit themselves so that they are poor in everything. When they limit themselves they close the door to their own prosperity.
It is not wise to throw pearls to swine or to waste the ointment on those who will not allow you to approach them. Save the savable first so that you will increase in numbers and then with more and more of you, you can spread the energy and reach even the poor.
When I was here I was only one, then added twelve and then more and now you too must multiply. The more of you there are the more we can cover, the more we can spread the love of God. We will enrich the world and we must start with you and it must start with love.
You may encounter opposition, doubt, fear and disbelief but persevere. The Holy Spirit will pave the way and bridge the gap.
Your work is cut out for you. But your armor is my presence in your life. Know that wherever you are, I am. Wherever we are together, we will manifest the glory of God.

Love from the Master,
Jesus

On evil

Jesus comes to say this,
Good is stronger than any problem, any wrong.
Love is more powerful than any evil.
Man defines and evaluates evil, not God.
Man uses social structures, social customs and social mores to define evil. What man calls evil at one stage he calls right at another.
God alone is in a position to see good in all because He sees all from a different perspective than man does. He sees all developing and growing and on different levels and therefore man should not judge on appearances alone.
Last night, you were discussing a man who you thought was not spiritual because he had been married five times. A man having had five wives may have treated each one of them more magnificently than one man treats one wife. God sees how the love is used and how each gives to the other.
Man looks only at laws and customs. Man does need laws to survive, but laws must be understood in the context of love and understanding. The way that each treats the other is the only law that God knows. If there is love, compassion, understanding, forgiveness, then God is pleased.
You are all children of God. Be happy. All will glow with God's love and the earth will be saved with love.
Blessings to you all.

Love from the Master,
Jesus

On sin

Jesus comes to say this,
Sin is the separation of the self from God.
Denying your potential and failing yourself is the real sin.
For to deny yourself is to deny the God who created you and to deny the perfection which He is capable of creating.
People with false modesty think they are putting themselves down, but it is the God who created them they are insulting, for God does not create inferiority.
All is holy to God and all is lovable.
The real sin is not to know your connection with perfection.

Love from the Master,
Jesus

On man's effect on God's design

Jesus comes to say this,

The light of God shines and the world sees it not. Be assured that God loves the world and everything in it. Man does not see the design of God's world. Everything in it has a purpose. Each thing was created to fill a need. But each blemish on God's creation was put there by man. Weeds are a result of imbalance and this imbalance goes into the cells inherited by the seeds.

Everything God created was once beautiful. It is only time and man that has given you weeds. Man refuses to take responsibility but the responsibility is his. You are now living in the twentieth century. There are thousands of years of mutations. Every time man stepped on a flower or broke a branch or bent a twig he changed God's order. Now you have undesirable plants, animals and insects and want to blame God for them.

How do you explain the weather? Doesn't God control the weather?

No. God gave you the elements of weather. Man has mutated the streams and rivers, the atmosphere. God sent rain, sun and wind. They were all to work together but the cycles have been disturbed. The patterns have been changed by man. Can you put blue dye into water and expect the water not to be blue?

Man is so reluctant to take the blame for what he has done or could do. It is easy to blame God. Man can make the world beautiful if he begins to have reverence for life, if he understands that everything has a purpose and with this knowledge uses things wisely, with love.

Man must realize that the only motivating force must be love. Today men are ruled by intellect rather than the heart. Emotions like anger, rage, hatred and resentments are more important than caring, love and affection. When will the world be ready to understand? A messiah who performs miracles is not the answer. You must all begin to understand God loves you. You must love each other. There is no other way.

Life is beautiful if only you do not fight it. Remember the words of the Master: The light of God surrounds the world. Some of you may be in the shadows but you may all wander into the light any time you choose and you and I will meet and embrace and go to see the Father of all and He will set you free. That is the way. Find the truth that will bring you to me. I am always waiting and I love you all.

Love from the Master,

Jesus

On the energy crisis

Jesus comes to say this,

All of the problems we face in the world today are problems that can be solved. All it takes is awareness and application.

People today become frightened at a lack of this or a change of that, but the world has always had problems and they have always been solved.

Do you think the energy crisis you have today is any more severe than the energy crisis before the discovery of electricity? Was it not just as much a problem to have to depend on candles for light and fire for energy? Then electricity was discovered — I say discovered because electricity was already existing just as all kinds of energy exist now waiting to be discovered.

The only elements that need to be added are man's initiative, man's goodness and man's purpose.

When men put their trust in the higher power we call God there is no problem that can not be solved for God is love and perfect love casts out fear and without fear, men can live in peace and harmony and in joy and in love.

It is just a matter of degree but all problems have existed before and all problems have been solved before.

Trust in the goodness of men everywhere to emerge triumphant and to use their talents wisely and all will partake of the kingdom of God.

Be blessed in the work of the Father and in the love of the son, Jesus.

Love from the Master,
Jesus

On concern about money

Jesus comes to say this,

The fear of not having money is a real one, but money alone is not food, is not clothing, does not cover you in a storm. It is what money does that is important.

Money allows people to interact with each other and to buy goods and services. If people were to give goods and services, there would be no use for money.

Of course, the world has "progressed" to the point where every material good and every service costs money and that is frightening. If you have no money you will have to rely on something to get through — either yourselves, each other or God. You will survive. It is what you do with your survival that is important. If it brings you closer to God, you will be one of the lucky ones. If not, you start all over again. Don't let it frighten you. Disaster, financial or otherwise, is only for those who want it or need it in order to fulfill their learning goals.

If people would only place faith in themselves, live fully according to God's design and God's love, remove their guilts and love one another, there would be no need for these lessons.

You have too many among you who don't understand God's love. Be sure in the love of God. Even in all things, material, physical, whatever.

Those who have their sights on their source and live accordingly will survive. Be free of worry about economics. It's just journalism talk. Don't let it get to you. God is always in charge of your life and that is all that matters.

Love from the Master,
Jesus

On fear and worry

Jesus comes to say this.

All of the time that man spends in fear and worry should be spent in love and forgiveness. It is so difficult for man to see what is at the root of his disease. Whether it is psychological or physical is no matter. The real disease is the closing up of the heart to the flow of God's love.

So many who go to church and profess a particular religion feel that that is all that is necessary. The real message of God is to love one another and forgive one another. Let the flow of the God power go through you for this is the way to replenish the earth.

God is the source of all and all is of God. Why do you celebrate the birth of Jesus and not remember the teachings of the Christ?

Believe, have faith, be one with God, be one with the universe for all are one. All are brothers and this is the way to recognize God. See Him in each of you. Be sure that when you love each other you create the love that will save the world.

Yet there are those who will ask, how can this happen? Work in your own little corner, in your own little place. If you project love where you are you will make it grow around you.

Look at the life of Christ. He only did what he had to do and was what he had to be and love was the result.

Be what you are, where you are and love will grow.

Come to the Father for everything.

Love from the Master,
Jesus

On fear of lack

Jesus comes to say this,
As you look to this day, find your connection with the force that you call God, each in his own way.
Look to this morning, to this noon, to this evening and know that the force that you identify with as the power in your lives manifests in its own way, in its own rhythm, in its own time. If you are aware that it is there with you, you will be able to meet anything, you will be able to do anything.
If only each one of you was aware of the love that God has for you, you would see how simple life is.
You are much in danger of becoming victims of the people who are using scare techniques to cause you concern. Don't let it happen.
There is power in the universe.
There is transportation in the universe.
There is food in the universe.
Do not listen to those who travel in fear of the end of supply. God's supply is endless and those of you who travel as children of God will see the supply.
The energy of God comes in many forms and in many ways. Keep open to the possibility of the new, to change, to development, to discovery and do not travel in fear. Do not accept limits. God loves you. Must you love yourselves less than God loves you?
Be open and receptive to all. Serve God in His time and in His way.

Love from the Master,
Jesus

On going to the Father for our needs

Jesus comes to say this,

The world is beginning to blossom. The buds are beginning to stir. This is a time for rebirth. You will learn the lesson of faith and trust from nature.

Each seed that struggles to burst its shell does so because it is in its nature to do so. Each sapling, each bulb, each root pushes forth because it was designed to do so.

So too does man have a purpose and a design and possesses all in him that is necessary to flower. If man would only recognize this and stop pushing against his nature he can fulfill the law.

God is love. He created in love. He nourishes in love. All man has to do is to accept that love and rejoice.

Does the Father choose what to supply?

No, you choose. You choose by faith believing you will have it. Then let God decide the time and place.

How about unanswered prayers?

Remember that you are not in a position to judge other people's prayers. Sometimes people outwardly pray for something they inwardly deny because they do not have the courage to accept what God will freely give them. Then they say God will not answer prayers.

How about praying for someone else's healing?

People are awed by disease and illness. They look to God as the cause and the cure. The cause and the cure is in your own mind. If you pray for the recovery of another you must be sure that person wants recovery. Sometimes disease is a way to escape the responsibility of living.

What about accidents?

Accidents are events. They happen and are lessons. They are caused by energies, positive and negative energies, that battle for expression. One need not have accidents if one lives according to the law. If you disrupt the balance of positive and negative energies you cause things to happen. The balance is disturbed by lack of inner harmony and spreads to include others. Whoever is the strongest willed can disturb the harmony for others. That is why it is important to control your own destiny — your own mind. Never let anyone take control of you or your thoughts in any way. What you give, give freely but always keep control of your choice.

I think we are beginning to explain life as God meant it to be.

Love from the Master,
Jesus

On judging by appearances

Jesus comes to say this,
 Be one with the Father in all you do. There is nothing on earth that the Father can not handle and does not control but man thinks he is the one who pushes the buttons.
 God is the source and all comes from God. Unless you know this and live accordingly you miss the joy of living and the beauty of life.
 Man judges by appearances and runs his life that way. A child of God runs his life in faith knowing the Father would never send him trials he could not handle. Sometimes trials seem out of proportion but that is only because you see only the outer manifestations and judge accordingly. God sees the whole and knows the whole and knows the potential.
 Many of you who doubt your own ability deny your potential and retreat rather than go forward. When you deny your inner being you have frustration, anger, resentment and pain. If man would get his eyes back on the source he would live every moment to the fullest. Of course, this takes time but this is what growth is — allowing the inner spirit to be and unfold and reveal its potential.
 Age is no factor. This can happen at sixteen or at sixty. Pansies are planted in the spring and tulips are planted in the fall. Each unfolds its inner beauty at the right time.
 Men of little faith have little faith in themselves and in the goodness of God. If they did, they would realize their places in the design and would be at peace and know the joy of God.

Love from the Master,
Jesus

On the breaking of habits

Jesus comes to say this,

Before one tries to remove an old habit, one must discover what purpose that habit serves. Sometimes a habit, even a bad one, prevents something far worse from occurring. Smoking cigarettes may be preventing a larger breakdown of emotions that are more difficult to deal with.

The real road to health is not in eliminating the undesirable as much as it is in acquiring the desirable. The desirable is one's attitude about life, one's attitude about health, one's ability to cope with life.

And, the necessary ingredient is faith.

Trust that God knows what is best, that God will supply what is best, that what is good for you will eventually be yours.

The problem is that people see only the limits, and they reach only for the smallest and when this does not satisfy they find something to blame or some excuse for doing things they know they should not be doing.

If one is complete in his feeling about himself and about his relationship to God and to other people, he falls into a serenity, a peace, a tranquility where nothing else is needed. Food, cigarettes, liquor, whatever is no longer necessary. That is the only way to be rid of an old habit which is undesirable.

Finding yourself, finding your peace is the way.

Jesus says, I am the light, the truth, and the way. Only by me can you come to the Father. Only by following the truths of your being, which is the Christ in you, can you come to the Father, which is peace. With God, you need nothing to ease you because you have ultimate peace.

People look on habits as causes. They are not causes, they are results. They are symptoms. When you are complete in the spirit, any habit which is unnecessary will fall away. BUT the road is not easy. It requires an understanding of the self, the acceptance of the self, an awareness of the importance of the self, and growth of the self.

Once you feel your oneness with the God force, all that is unnecessary falls away and you are in the spirit, and in perfect peace and harmony.

But it is not easy.

Especially, in your world where too much of the world is with you. Too much abundance makes you aware of lack.

But those who follow the Christ within will see the way, the truth and the light.

Be blessed in the Lord of all which is within you.

Love from the Master,

Jesus

On the brotherhood of man

Jesus comes to say this,

All of life is part of God. To know that you are all part of the same loving force makes you all one.

It doesn't matter if one worships in Bangkok or India or Peking, China or Brooklyn, New York. Each man that bows down his head to pray thinks he is contacting God. Then why do you think only those who know Christ can be saved? The Christ is in all men. God is for all men.

Believe that the Father loves all. Once you realize that you are all brothers you will have compassion and love for each other. The other is just a matter of geography, but all spirits are God's and there is no geography.

For God, it is all here and all now. All are part of the kingdom of God.

Call any man brother and you serve God.

But beware. It is sometimes far easier to call a stranger brother than members of your own family. Your responsibility is to take care of your own little world — your spouse, your children, your parents, your bosses, the people you work with. Call them brother and start there with forgiveness, compassion and love.

If each does that the ripples will start to expand and grow and encircle the earth.

A leaf can not fall in New Haven without being felt in London. You are all part of the same cosmic order. But each of you is responsible for his own little space. Making your space beautiful is all you need do. The rest will happen.

Come to the realization that God loves you and you are all His children.

Be blessed in the love of the Father. In my Father's house, there are many mansions and rooms for each of you. Don't go out of your own little mansion unless you put on the cloak of love, understanding, forgiveness and acceptance.

Be blessed in the Father's love and rejoice. Goodbye for now.

Love from the Master,

Jesus

On recognizing one's own talent

Jesus comes to say this,
The power of God is in every living thing. The love of God is to recognize this fact. When you look upon the faces of all around you and see God showing forth you have conquered the world and have become lord of your own private kingdom.

This is the heaven of which you speak and it is there, free for each of you.

How wonderful it is when you tune into what is the real you — the self created by God to serve Him with all of the talents He has given you.

It is so easy to look at another and envy him. The truth is you all have some exclusive talent which is yours alone and if you use it in the service of the Lord it grows and grows. The joy is to recognize your own talent and use it to serve God.

You think talents are those of a good singing voice or the ability to paint or the power to build or to make music. Being a good mother is a talent, being able to take charge of social gatherings is a talent, knowing how to shop and use money is a talent, if they are done to serve God. By serving God you serve man.

Every action you use is a talent peculiar only to you and when you couple it with the desire to serve God it becomes the power of God working through you and that is what makes you a star or a champion.

Serving God in the world is the only true career. The wages you earn because of this are incidental. It is how you do your job that is important.

Everyone is dependent on everyone else and herein lies the peace of God. Knowing that no one can take your place you must not try to manage every place. It takes every stitch to make a garment not just the last stitch.

Be at peace. God loves you. The time will come when you can show that you love God.

Love from the Master,
Jesus

On anger

Jesus comes to say this,
A way of dealing with the problem of handling anger is to not say anything. You will remember that when they taunted me and led me from Pilate to the mob I could have shouted defenses and vindictives but when you are secure in your own little kingdom you are king. Therefore, you must act like a king, not like the mob.
To put it in your terms don't waste your energy battling with something that you can not defeat. Preserve your own sense of Christ — retire into your kingdom, find an impenetrable space and remain there until the other person stops or leaves.
All you are doing is fighting for your ego — and the way to fight for your ego is to preserve it, not fragment it and give it away piece by piece.

Are you saying, don't argue at all?
Yes, that is the way to win your own integrity, your own self-esteem. Anger will never win.
If you keep your serenity you will always be the victor, the master, the king. That keeps you in control of yourself and others must bow down before that serenity.
It is the easiest way of all if you remember that I will come and help you if you call me. I will strengthen your ability to keep silent.
Your ego is not that important because when you give up the ego you will get your self and that is the better of the two.
You will see better days, believe — it will be so.

Love from the Master,
Jesus

On suicide

Jesus comes to say this,

It is difficult to lose a member of the family or a friend by suicide, but there should be no grieving for the one who has left. He is only doing what he feels is right to do and he alone bears the consequences. He is still on a path to God even though we may not understand his timetable or his means.

Do not see suicide as a tragedy. Do not see any death as a tragedy. See tragedy in those who live without meaning, without joy, without progress. The ultimate is to live life with complete confidence in God and in self.

I know those left behind will grieve but they grieve for their loss, not for the soul who has started his approach to God and is one step nearer his goal of completeness and fulfillment.

Send prayers and healing to the family that they see the passing in its true light and be examples to others who do not know the new consciousness that God's love makes possible.

What happens to souls who commit suicide?

Souls who commit suicide must come back and face the same problem over again until it is resolved. It is not easy for them because when they pass over the problem is still with them for the mind brings with it all its stored memories and you create from it the space you live in.

Most of the souls who "kill" themselves have the reason for wanting to leave the earth plane still current in their memories therefore they are still living it.

There are a few who commit suicide who are able to drop the idea as soon as they pass over. It is the awareness of yourself in the space you have, in relation to God, that is significant — not how you die. It doesn't matter to God how or when you die if you are further along on your evolution.

It takes much development to be able to create a happy environment if you leave life prematurely because of the love for those you leave behind and because of jobs left undone. Not many souls are this advanced and therefore when they get "here" they are in torment. Those who commit suicide to save others or help others can make the transition more peacefully but all will eventually work for good.

But remember, God does not forsake anyone. You are all part of God and for Him to forsake or discard any one of you is to discard Himself. You must believe that God is love. Love is forgiving, accepting, supporting, helping and understanding. Can't you believe that God is these things?

He is all to all. It is you who create your own heaven or hell.

Love from the Master,

Jesus

On sudden death

Jesus comes to say this,
Let the events of yesterday be yesterday. There is today to live in. Those who do not understand this will continue to ask, Why? There is no answer. It is just an event. No one is to blame. It was just the perspective of the soul involved. He will grow in spirit and move into awareness after death rather than before.
It is the reaction to the event that is important. The point is it doesn't matter how life ends on the earth plane, because it does not end in spirit. It is how one reacts to that that makes peace both for those here and those who go on.
It is difficult for you to understand because we cannot prove to you scientifically that life goes on but in faith believing you can find this peace. Do not mourn those who pass over. Learn from their absence the presence of God always, everywhere and you need not feel sad.
You ask why this particular person or family. The question is academic. Events are events. They happen because of the breaking of natural and physical and spiritual laws. But nothing is that final that God's love can not set it right.
Rejoice in the beauty and wisdom of God's love and laws. All is now. All is forever. Be at peace.

Love from the Master,
Jesus

On a design for life

Jesus comes to say this,
The fear of death is man's biggest fear. He clings to life because he fears the unknown at the end of life. If he only understood it is all the same. Life is eternal. It is just a different form. But eternal life places a responsibility on the individual. It forces him to look at himself, and weigh his present actions in the light of eternity. That is difficult for him because then his present actions must be carefully selected. In order to reach eternal life every lesson must progress you.

Step by step weed out those qualities which shut out love such as the fears, the anxieties, the doubts which make us suspicious of others rather than loving and sharing.

It is not enough to hand someone money or goods. What matters is the sharing of feelings, the sharing of fears, of loneliness, of time, of joys, of tears. Man wants to touch another and know that he is noticed, not as a statistic or a stereotype but as a separate entity, as a "one" expressing himself in the only way he knows how.

Man basically is good. He does not want to steal or plunder or harm others. It is only when his original design is tampered with that he reaches for a way to be and sometimes he thinks that the answer lies in stealing or having power over others. The truth is that he who has power over himself first, automatically influences others.

A master is in charge of himself, not others. A master controls himself, not others. A master loves others because they are himself. To be one with God makes you one with all that is. All that is is you and all that is is yours. This may not be any religion but it is truth.

You could not expect less from the God who is all love.

Love from the Master,
Jesus

On the purpose of life

Jesus comes to say this,

The purpose of life is to learn.

It takes situations and events and people to bring the lessons.

You should always ask yourself, What is this situation trying to teach me?

Don't be afraid to let the answer come through. It is this answer which will bring the healing.

Your answers may be one word answers like patience, tolerance, freedom, love, faith, trust — or words like freedom from fear, removal of anger.

The lessons teach you to refine your self. They do not change others. They do not change the world but your world will change as your self creates a newer reality for you, and many of you operating in this way will create a newer world, a peaceful world, a loving world. The world you live in need not be negative and it need not be fearful if as many of you as possible live in a reality of love.

How should we interact with those on a different level of consciousness?

By being an example. By not giving energy to the negative. By blessing the negative and thanking God for its lesson.

If you eliminate rain, you will have no flowers. But rain alone does not bring flowers. It takes seeds and soil and sun and air.

The negative alone is worthless but to eliminate it does not bring growth. Growth needs the seed of thought, the soil for the thought to grow, the sun and air for nourishment. Then you will have the flowering of awareness and insight into truth. But truth once yours embraces all negatives, all situations, all life and makes of your journey through life a joy.

Be aware that God loves you. No one is excluded from God's graces, only those who exclude themselves.

Love from the Master,

Jesus

On why one becomes ill

Jesus comes to say this,

Illness, no matter how severe or of what kind, is only a manifestation of a need of the spirit. Some will not allow their spirits to be healed, therefore the physical body reflects this. Some people need to cling to physical illness to protect them from something else which would be more painful to face.

How can you justify this in a three year old boy with bronchitis?

If you realize that every soul has within it an inner source of knowledge, it is clear. The inner self of that child knows why it chooses bronchitis over health. We as adults may find this difficult to believe. If you study infants you will see them grow according to an inner blueprint even from the moment of birth and before. That spirit subconsciously knows what lesson it is seeking.

Children who are born with disease or who have accidents know in the deep recesses of their minds why they are choosing that lesson or that avenue of expression. If there is enough love around the infant he may learn and he may overcome. You see many instances of loving parents with handicapped children where the problem becomes an asset. There are others whose parents deal in fear and anxieties and anger and bitterness and the child reacts to those the way he can. You must remember that the physical body is only a machine. The spirit may be growing healthier and more beautiful day by day until there is no limitation of the physical.

Parents find this hard to accept. They think tears and fears are the expression of love. Disattachment is love. Allowing that child to suffer and cleanse himself of his lesson is love. That spirit is here for his soul growth and he alone must handle his life and his death as well as his birth. I know this is a difficult concept.

Deal with each situation differently. Learn from each situation separately. Give parents hope and comfort. The rest must be in them or must come to them as part of their growth.

Your prayers will help. All prayers help but you are still dealing with the need of the person's spirit to express whatever is in him that is causing difficulty. I hope you understand and can go on from here with a new insight. Keep healing. Keep sending healing thoughts.

Be blessed in God's work.

Love from the Master,

Jesus

On the continuity of animal life

Jesus comes to say this,
All life is spirit. Life is in every cell, no matter how minute. Every cell has its own intelligence whether it is in animal, vegetable or human being.
If all life is spirit, then all is of God. God sees the spirit in animals and knows the spirit in animals. How could you doubt this?
Each kind of animal develops according to a set plan. Each mates with its own. You call it instinct, but that is just a word. Semantics, to explain the Christlike activity of animals.
Think of your little dog. Doesn't she behave according to whatever inner thing guides her? You can't force her to bark when she doesn't want to. She asks for water according to her inner need and eats when her inner needs express this desire for food. Is she any different than you or your children?
When you become aware that animals have been created by God with the same precision and love and caring used to create all life you will see the spirit of God in every living thing.

Do animals have continuity of life?
Life is continuity because it is Now. It is always. It has no beginning and no end. Animals incarnate as their need arises. They continue on in the love shared between master and pet. Wherever you have an exchange of love, life goes on. Life is. Life does not fade.
The key is love. Love is the thing that holds together every cell of every form of life. In a strong love bond, an animal may choose to stay close to a person even after the death of its body because love is the strongest bind in the world.
Now, I know you are puzzled about killing animals. Remember, that the seed must give up its life in order to become a plant. It is also true of animals. Some of them must give up their lives to make life for others. This is not contrary to God's plan. All has its purpose. All has its place. All is loved by God for finding its journey and its path with love.
Man does not understand this and makes all kinds of judgments and edicts to try to understand and ends up misunderstanding. Since you can not kill the spirit, it makes no difference how the body of the animal is used.
All is spirit. All is love. All is continuous. All goes on and if one sees with the eyes of love in every situation, then one understands.

What about when one is not able to love?
Ah, but that is your journey through life. To learn. You have no choice. You must learn, however long it takes you. You

must allow each to be what he was designed to be. You may not like behavior and you may not understand a personal behavior, but you must allow him to be what his design has made him whether animal, vegetable or human.

All has a purpose. You would find it difficult to live with a lion, but you must allow him to be a lion while you remain human. That is the essence of God. That is love. If you do this you will understand that all life is now. All life is love. That all is God's plan and design and all works for good.

That is why you must not judge for you don't know why or what each purpose is. Be centered in your inner feelings and you will not go wrong even if you are still on a level which requires a lot of learning. The old saying that God will not send you what you can not handle is true. Each develops according to his level of understanding and can only live at that level of understanding whether it is the way you deal with animals or the way you deal with brothers and sisters.

We could go into a much deeper philosophical discussion but just remember that all is love and love is God and God is spirit. Spirit has no beginning and no end. It is.

Be blessed.

Love from the Master,
Jesus

On forgiveness

Jesus comes to say this,
   The way one looks at Easter determines the ability to heal the self.
   If one sees only the crucifixion one sees man as a sinner, who has to rely on Jesus to save him. Therefore, he sees himself as unworthy, evil, always doing wrong. It also allows man to go on doing wrong because there is always the savior.
   If one sees not the crucifixion but the resurrection he knows that he is responsible for his choices but that no matter how many wrong choices he makes, there is always an Easter Sunday, a new beginning, a new birth — all is a birth into eternal happiness for God is giving the chance to try again and all is forgiven.
   If God forgives, then we must forgive ourselves — we must forgive the inadequacy, the inefficiency, the fears, the guilt, the little child in us who was obstinate, hurt and broken. And in forgiving all we can love all and this is the first step to healing.
   Forgiving ourselves for not being perfect is the first step to healing. Loving ourselves is the second step and loving others is the completion of healing.
   Jesus was the teacher but the people were slow in learning. Be your own priest and think for yourself.
   All is of God. God forgives. God loves. Man should do no less.

Does God judge those who commit murder?
   If God is forgiving why should he not forgive all? What would be the point of mercy if it were selective? What would be the point of hope if there were no hope?
   You might think that this would license anyone to kill but the reverse would be true. It is only envy, jealousy, passions, greed that cause killing. When every man realizes that he can have everything from the Father, killing others is not relevant. When one has all — the love, the peace, the joy — there is no need for anything else. I know this is a difficult concept — just remember that time is irrelevant. There is no death. With no death, what other significance would violence have?
   Forgiving is the first step to healing. Forgive yourself. Forgive others. Each is only being what he was created to be. There should be no guilt in man, only love.
   Have a good day. Be happy. Spring comes and new dreams, new hopes, Easter every morning.

Love from the Master,
Jesus

On reincarnation

Jesus comes to say this,
When a soul chooses to reincarnate there is usually a reason. He senses the need to do so or senses a need to be with others who have reincarnated who may need him. It is not always necessary to incarnate but it takes a very strong and very developed soul who can create his world and continue to grow only on the spirit side. Also, it takes longer. There is opportunity on the earth level to learn to serve others.

Many souls choose to return even though they are very highly developed because their desire to help others is so great, and because they feel they have a quality the world might need. Some come back in error because of a false pride.

If you understand that it is when you feel the peace and love of God totally and fully you understand your place in the universe and you make your choices in line with the will of God for you. If God needs you for a particular service you may choose to incarnate to fulfill that special function as Mahatma Gandhi did. The choice is always yours and you may choose to incarnate or not as you wish, but your motive must always be to serve God and to serve others, to love God and to love others. You can do the same kind of work on both sides of the veil and that is what is important.

Is it possible to incarnate only once?
Yes. Some of your great masters did and grew in spirit. Some even though they had achieved that growth still came back to help mankind.

Why are there more souls on earth now?
There are not. It only seems so because you are more adept at keeping records and spreading news. Who of you knows how many people inhabited the plains of South Africa or South America at a time before computers and calculators? Anthropologists try to estimate but they do it only by guessing and speculating and most of your imagination is spurred by Hollywood studios. None of you really knows what the world was a million years ago. Many of you may have been here then and some of you have not progressed very far in all that time. Others have become masters and adepts and have known the love of God first hand.

The important thing is the journey of the soul whatever way it chooses. That is the free will that God will not take away from you and which you can use at any time. Once you are in touch with the inner master you will know what is best for you and how you want to accomplish it. Some of you may not incarnate for thousands of years and then see a need to return while others may try to come back immediately. It is your

perception of yourself which rules your decision and the choice is always yours.
  You are part of the God force but you are yourself. See it as if you were a drop of rain. You would fall, nourish the ground, help produce a flower, then return to a cloud. No one could pick you out of the cloud but you are there and you could come down to earth again or you could remain part of the cloud. You are one and yet part of the whole. Does that explain to you the God you are part of? You are going very deep in wondering about this question and it can not be explained easily.

Why do we have no memory of past lives?
  Because it is not necessary. If it were necessary it would come to you. Your role is to deal with the Now. Always deal with the Now with the highest and the best that is in you and you will understand it all — because the arms of God would enfold you and you would know His presence. Many have. It is hard to express it to another.
  Let's let it go at that for now.

Love from the Master,
Jesus

On karma

Jesus comes to say this,
  I don't like the word, karma. It implies a scapegoat — it gives a reason — it provides a copout.
  We are all responsible for our choices, and we are all on our own spiritual journey. To blame other situations for a way of life we accept is no different than saying God is punishing you by placing you in a particular situation.
  Each problem is growth producing but it is too simple to say you must stay in a situation because it is karmic.
  Each person grows according to his own needs and abilities. The choices must be individual ones but based on love — love of self, love of fellow man, love of God.
  Love of self does not force you to stay in a situation because it is karmic. It teaches you what to extract from that situation, use it and go on. The real test is being able to let go and let God work.
  If you keep your eyes on the source, nothing is impossible and karma is just a word.
  Your strength comes from God but the choice is yours. Do you understand that sentence? Your strength comes from God but you decide when and where and how to use God's strength and love.
  You can wallow in self pity or you can rise above all of it. It is the resurrection which is important not the crucifixion.
  Karma is no different than saying, It's God's will that you suffer. We have already agreed that God does not punish.
  You are your own worst enemies. God loves you. God is all love. Remember also that the old Indian philosophies were man's attempt at that stage of evolution to deal with the meaning of life, man and God. It does not mean that all they teach is necessarily the best way or the only way. If Vedanta is not your bag, let it go — I rather enjoy having you in my *corner.*
  Blessings from the Father of all and from your humble Master. All of the wisdom of the universe does not equal the wisdom in your own mind as to what is best for you.

Love from the Master,
Jesus

On dredging up the past

Jesus comes to say this,
It is not necessary to dig up the past in order to be healed. To do so sometimes becomes an end in itself and becomes an excuse for all your imperfections, all your hurts, your pains.
Jesus never asked how did you become lame or how did you become blind. It didn't matter. He just healed. What is important is that you accept all that you are in the Now. All that has shaped you, all that has led to what you are. Realize that you chose that path for yourself. If you were to use it well you would see each stage of your life as an adding on and the past is only a part of Now. The past is not in control of your future if you are in control of yourself. Herein lies real healing.

What about habits?
This applies. If you take control of each Now in the best way you can, if you are master, if you are Christ, you will eventually change any habit. But deal with it in the present always.
Some people on different levels need someone to take charge of them. That is why Jesus was cast in the role of savior. No one, not even the best therapist there is, can save you if you do not become your own master. For those on lower levels there are those who can help. The fact that people go to psychoanalysts for years shows that dredging up the past of itself is no solution. They are still counting on the doctor to save them, rather than saving themselves.
When Jesus was on the cross or before Pilate, he never asked Why am I here? What in my past brings me here to this place? He said, Forgive them for they know not what they do. Whoever created a trauma in you was only acting on whatever level of consciousness he was and if you forgive all that, you heal yourself.
There are those who need to be led and those who like to be leaders, but a disciple of the Christ is master of himself and allows everyone to be at whatever level he is without becoming his master. Don't be God for anyone else. The best disciple of Jesus is an example and an inspiration, not a mother figure or a father substitute.
It does no good to know your karma if it gives you an excuse to go on having your faults and being ineffective. Forgiving the past and starting each day in the glory of the resurrection is to have learned the message of Jesus.
You have been led from before you were born to reach this point by me and by your guardian angel and by your inner Christ.

Love from the Master,
Jesus

On the growth of the soul

Jesus comes to say this,
The purpose of life is to grow closer to God, to realize your spiritual nature and to try to live in such a way that everything that happens to you is a lesson that teaches you the love and power of Infinite Intelligence. Knowing that life is an area where we are experiencing events in order to perfect the spirit allows us to keep perspective and to avoid making judgments which interfere with soul growth.

As a soul becomes aware of its relationship to God, it strives to become more in tune with the natural laws that it may have perfect attunement with that Divine Force we call God. Every avenue of expression is a way for learning, every event is a place for growth, every day is an opportunity for unfolding. We look for our place in God's plan and when we find this we have the peace of God for we know that what is ours will come to us. We work in perfect harmony with our fellow man as well as those who have passed on for all are part of the kingdom of God and it is through this mutual concern that we grow and develop according to God's holy plan for us.

The purpose of life is to know God, to love God, and to serve God in this world and in the next. This is not always easy but it should be the goal of everyone to make the journey through life knowing that God is in control and our purpose is to return to that Godhead from whence we came.

One of the major ways to do this is to realize who is your neighbor and to live as though every man is your brother. All men were created by God and meant to live in peace and harmony. You will come to the realization of God through serving man, for man is in the material world and is dependent upon other men. Once he realizes this he will see God in each creature and by loving all he loves the Prime Force, the Divine Wisdom, the Infinite Love we call God. Any questions?

Is there a spirit world?
Yes. The spirit world is just like your world. People are the same. They don't all suddenly change just because they pass over. They have the same personalities, the same characters they had on earth. As they progress up the ladder of learning they realize that thought is all that is necessary to create the world they want. They can have homes, schools, opera houses, whatever suits them. The sad thing is that they choose exactly what they had while on earth. They stick to what they know rather than reaching out for more, for better.

Children grow in wisdom and mature but there is no aging as such. There is joy, peace and love except for those who carry their earthbound experiences with them. That is why it is a

good idea to get rid of any bad habits while on earth so that time will be better used in spirit.
Everything operates on love and helping others is the prime vocation. That is why Spirit likes to return to speak to those on the earth plane because spirits progress by helping those on the material plane.
All work towards complete attunement to the Father for this is the ultimate joy.
All God's children are entitled to Paradise.

Love from the Master,
Jesus

On finding joy in marriage

Jesus comes to say this,

Do not fall in love before you have loved yourself. For to do so is only to give another person the power to bring joy to you. Nothing or no one can bring you joy. It must be within you.

When you find this unity within you, you will love. When you meet the person who fills the other side of you you will love with respect, with sharing, with concern for each other's growth and welfare. This is the love to strive for, for this is God's joy and this that God — God love, God joy, God wisdom — shall unite no man shall put asunder.

This is marriage, the meeting of two minds that grow together toward one common goal off in the distance that looks inviting to them — because it is the Christ light which beckons every human soul.

So many take their eyes off the goal and see only the obstacles and bypass the joy that God promised.

Our young people need to know that they have a right to pursue this Christ light and to dare to dream — for all they want is available from God. What they want is peace, love, joy, hope and fulfillment. These do not come from materialism but from mutual respect, caring, loving and sharing. This is the kingdom of God and you may all have it. It is within you.

All are alike. All can prosper. All can love. Look to your own mind. Do not blame the past or fear the future. Learn the Now. Learn in the Now. Do not blame others but take responsibility for your own dream and make it come true. The dream is not important but the pursuit of it is. The fulfilling of the dream is divine right but the growth comes from the pursuit.

That you be in the right place at the right time is not chance, but if you keep following your dream you will be where you are meant to be and you will see divine right descend upon you as a white dove of fulfillment and blessing.

You are all part of the kingdom of God. Rejoice!

Love from the Master,
Jesus

On abortion

Jesus comes to say this,
Every human soul is unique and every journey through life is different. Abortion is one avenue that God uses to allow a soul that is in doubt to reincarnate. The soul chooses a situation where he has a chance to reconsider. If the soul decides to reincarnate or changes its mind the inner self will tell the mother.

The souls who choose to reincarnate in this fashion are souls too recently passed and too confused. They must have this choice and this opportunity to change their minds. Some souls do not decide early enough and they will miscarry later in pregnancy.

No lost pregnancy should be mourned. No infant death should be mourned. The soul who is using the vehicle decided his fate. Sometimes an infant will live two or three days and then return to the Father. This is not to be thought of with sadness. It is only part of the journey of that soul.

At that moment of conception a soul has the opportunity to reincarnate. It is not a random choice however. The soul is aware beforehand of the situation it wishes to be in and waits for that opportunity — sometimes for years, sometimes only a short while. When the union takes place the soul can use it to start his new journey.

You see, in God's eyes there is no death. What you label misfortunes are only lessons on the road to God. Dying to your world is a joy — the age does not matter. Time is irrelevant here. One day or ninety years is significant only in how close one gets to the Father. If this concept were only understood, man would be so much more relaxed and open to life.

All works for good. All works for God. God loves you all.

Love from the Master,
Jesus

On further clarification of abortion

Jesus comes to say this,
The subject of abortion is very simple if you see the soul as an entity who is growing through centuries of time in an effort to reach perfection. When a soul decides to incarnate he looks for the situation where he at that stage of development thinks he will learn what he's after. Some souls pick a situation where the potential for an end to the pregnancy exists so that they may change their minds about incarnating at that time. If a soul accepts this conception and then decides to withdraw, it will impress the mother in such a way that she may choose abortion. Sometimes a mother may choose abortion and the soul will want to continue and her decision may be difficult.

You must remember that with the increased opportunity there are more souls attracted to conceptions who are not ready to incarnate and more reversals of choices. It is not serious, because each soul is responsible for its journey and its lesson and any problem it faces is only a process for growth.

Does this mean that God is not in charge of giving life?
No, remember the purpose is to get closer to God. God does control or inspire that desire to live and grow towards Him. God is life and the reason for life. Therefore, a soul chooses God when he chooses life. He loves God when he lives life. He serves God when he fulfills his purpose in life.

If he is not ready to start serving God he must wait until he is ready. The parents are only the instruments for his birth. All instruments are different and able to express their own wills. Their choices may not be wise ones or workable ones but that also is a lesson learned.

Remember, all souls are constantly progressing. Some slower than others, some less wisely than others but each finds his level of potential and works with it until he can progress higher.

Mothers who are in touch with themselves will be in tune with the problem of the soul's trying to incarnate through them and act accordingly. Not all are that progressed but the soul takes this risk when he makes this choice.

If you love and serve one another these problems are not problems but avenues of expression. The point is that man should realize he is part of a greater structure than appears on the surface and it is all interwoven and that the purpose of life on earth is to progress in spirit.

Don't be disappointed in anything. All works for good.

Love from the Master,
Jesus

On adoption

Jesus comes to say this,
Souls who need a certain lesson in life pick the situation for that lesson. That lesson may be not knowing their real parents and living in a foster home or being adopted — sometimes as an infant, sometimes as an older child. That is part of the situation for that lesson.
Adoptive parents are led to the soul just as blood parents are. It is not wholly chance. The necessary ingredients for the lesson must be present for that soul's growth.
Sometimes these children want to find their blood relatives but that is only after much has been worked out in the situation.
People say that adopting a child is dangerous because you don't know how it will turn out. It doesn't matter. It works out according to the lesson whether it is an adopted or natural child.

Why are there so many adolescent unwed mothers?
Because there is more opportunity for souls to be attracted to young people and because also this allows for incarnating and still finding adoptive parents.
Remember even adoptive parents had former lives and may know that soul from another life. They are not excluded from a relationship with that soul just because they are childless, any more than bachelors or single women are. All are part of former lives working on soul growth. What you see in this life is only this incarnation but includes all growth and all journeys.

What about childless couples?
That is their journey. The answer is — if one learns to trust in the will of God defined as peace and faith one sees all as part of whatever journey is there for each soul, whether mother, father or child. Do you understand?
Mother, father, child may all be from another incarnation still working together for soul growth.
Being an unwed mother is only a stigma of society. Creation, allowing the opportunity for a soul to incarnate who needs that lesson, is part of the overall pattern for all concerned.
Know that you will serve God in His time and in His way. Bless you for allowing the work of God to flow through you.

Love from the Master,
Jesus

On the importance of a mother's love

Jesus comes to say this,

The love of mankind starts with mothers. When mothers are understanding, children grow in love and are allowed to expand and be what God intended them to be. Every child is sent to your plane for a purpose. If only those who are responsible for the raising of children would see the Christ in them and allow it to express, love would return to the earth.

So many mothers think children must be trained just because they are smaller. Do you "train" a flower or a tree? All of God's creations express God if they are allowed to unfold. When they are free to do this, what is expressed is love.

The ten commandments are all summed up in that one word: Love. If you love each other how could you covet each other's belongings? How could you steal from someone you love?

On the other hand, if you discount any man as your brother then you can harbor malice and give him pain and you will get pain in return. If children don't learn love in their early years how can you expect them to become adults who treat each other with love?

Children of love must be out there in the market place where they can be an influence of love. They must permeate the atmosphere with love thoughts. They must spread it everywhere they go. How can we have more and more children of love? Only if we get the message to mothers and fathers.

Infants do not need money. They need caring, holding, touching, prayers — the light. Please believe this.

The salvation of the world is in your children. There are in your age many incarnating in wisdom. These new age children need to unfold and to express God. They must not be frustrated and belittled as in the past. Know that they do God's work and they try to bring the world back to God. These children are in the care of mothers — let these mothers take this responsibility seriously.

Life is more than training a child to live in society; it is preparing the soul to live in eternity.

It is time to start listening to children instead of constantly talking down to them or ignoring them altogether. I should have saved these comments until Mother's Day but what you should have is Children's Day and that day should be every day of the year.

The world needs to see my own live and grow in the love of God as shining examples of the light. There is no other way but through love. Mothers especially must raise children with love not just custodial care but a love for the unfolding and blossoming of the spirit within that is trying to express God.

Every child is a new flower in God's garden and while they can not all be roses there is room for lilacs and violets and lilies and even weeds. Remember, it is man who calls them weeds — what one calls a weed another calls a wildflower. A weed is only something that grows where it is not planned for and not wanted. If you decide you want it there it is no longer a weed but a living growing thing that might be more beautiful than you thought possible.

Keep God's world in order. Everything has a purpose and a design and all you must do is to allow it to express.

This doesn't mean that mothers must give up their individuality but only that each soul be allowed its "space" and there will be harmony and balance and God will be pleased.

God bless you all. Grow in the wisdom of God that the world may prosper. For now, goodbye.

Love from the Master,
Jesus

On the roles of mother and father

Jesus comes to say this,

The roles of mother and father in these days are no different than in any age. The child should find in parents support, love, understanding, freedom to grow, develop and unfold according to an inner need and an inner guidance.

Parents today put more stress on conforming to standards than allowing each child to be what he is. Competition between brothers and cousins makes tension.

Each child is unique and if a college education is not for him, he should not be compared to one who chooses college. If one wishes to be a laborer he should not be frowned upon but allowed to develop according to this plan, for the great plan of God is to provide avenues for each soul to serve and to grow according to God's design.

There are some who would separate the roles of father and mother but there is no difference. There are "chores" that men perform better than women but essentially both should learn to care, to nourish, to understand and to love the child. The child needs to know physical warmth and emotional understanding, not material needs only.

Fathers and mothers are caretakers only, not proprietors, for the child belongs to God and to himself not to the parents. The choices children make are what frees the adult in him but the adult is already there. The adult is inherent in every child. Many mothers and fathers forget this and struggle against odds to re-create what God has already created.

All children are born with the same potential. Some have imbalances but love will find a way to understand and deal with the situation. Too often fear and doubt take the place of love and there are problems. Too often parents are so wrapped up in self and their own problems that they don't see children as human beings and as gifts from the Father to the universe.

All has a purpose. All has a design. All works for good.

Love from the Master,
Jesus

On being a good parent

Jesus comes to say this,

When parents are given the responsibility for a new life they must see it as the avenue by which a soul makes its journey back to God. If they do, they will not be dismayed by the child's inability to live up to their expectations. They will see that the child is in communion with his creator and he will fulfill his purpose.

Unfortunately many of your people who become parents do not have this understanding and they bring children into the world and feel that they are the caretakers of that child's body and mind. They impose values and restrictions which close down the child's tie with God in the inner recesses of himself. The child spends the rest of his growth trying to find, one way or another, that sense of peace he subconsciously remembers. That is the cause of most of our unhappiness. That is the understanding that is needed to avoid problems with children later.

If you analyze parents' statements you will see that they deal with the effort of living in society, not with the development of the soul. If the soul develops in accordance with God's law, society will benefit and be easy to support.

Now what about all the situations now existing where this has not been done. The key word is expectations. If parents can be made to see that a child can not live up to expectations that are outwardly imposed but must be what he is ordained to be perhaps they would be able to relax and accept the child with love.

REMEMBER, every child is a soul that must sooner or later make his peace with God, not his parents. The parents are only the instruments for his life. Every child will be an adult who must recognize himself to survive. He must deal with his existence as he understands it and he cannot live for his parents.

Parents feel that because a child is doing this or that at age eight that he will always act age eight. Every infant born has no choice. He must grow — this is his purpose.

Now you ask me — what about autistic children, problem children? I must remind you that you see only what appears to be — autistic children, brain damaged children, problem children are still souls on their journeys to God.

Adults seem to think because they are older that they know everything for another but each soul is on its own journey. Some have rougher journeys than others and we don't understand that but the soul that is living that life does know in a deep recess of his being. He knows and his peace comes from living in harmony with that knowledge.

How do you present this idea to parents who are bewildered and confused about discipline and raising children?

By example, by support, by understanding, by realizing that each member of that problem is a different soul with a different problem and trying to work with each one in the problem on its own level. Do not think of anyone of them as having authority over another. Do not verbalize this but convey the idea that the child is responsible for his actions and he needs to learn from everything he does or doesn't do.

Use love, use support and above all, do not judge. You after all are also on your journey and are responsible only for your own growth in that you love and forgive and help those on another level in the way that you can.

You are all children of God, love one another.

Love from the Master,
Jesus

On marijuana

Jesus comes to say this:

Marijuana of itself is no more dangerous than any other thing that man gives control to. In some cases, less dangerous but man should not give control of his mind to anything, not even money. Being addicted to money is no different than being a user of marijuana.

Of course, this weed is not wholesome but neither are a lot of things that are fed children. The problem is not with the symptom but with the cause.

If children today or of any day were aware of being loved as infants in a warm physical understanding way they would not grow up to need drugs or alcohol or any artificial road to self-fulfillment.

There are those who smoke because they want to experiment with it. This has been true since time began.

There are those who desperately need to smoke it. In between, you have varying degrees of not being strong enough to refuse, and not wanting to refuse and just following the crowd. The sad thing is that young people do this to conform to each other but it makes them more isolated from each other.

Parents must realize that they can never understand this any more than they can understand the pressures on their children.

Each generation is different. Indeed each year is different. The significant thing is that each spirit learn to cope with his life on his level and learn from it and progress. There are always temptations. There is always the flesh in one way or another. That is what the spirit is learning.

No soul should give importance to any outside influence but when his spirit is weak he must grow in awareness to reach a level where he can do this. Don't condemn adolescents for this because there are many adults who do the same. The world focuses on adolescents because it feels it must "lead" them. The best way to do that is by example. If adolescents see the world as a wonderful place to be they will mature to be content within themselves and not need any outside thing.

Marijuana is just a word. It can be a substitute for any other word that describes man's need to find his inner Christ and does so by material means.

That marijuana is not a substitute for happiness is true. Adolescents don't expect to find happiness that way. It is just a reality of their existence just as saddle shoes and crew cuts were a reality of your adolescence.

Don't judge by the degree. All are the same. Each is a giving up of the mind to a control which is what the spirit must learn is wrong. Once a soul learns this, whether it is in adolescence or middle age, he can then open the door to the kingdom of heaven and know the peace of God.

Love your children. Understand their needs. Help them when they go wrong and know that they are on a journey to God and will follow many pathways to get to their destination. Just as all adolescents in all ages have done. I know this may not be a comfort when it is your child that is involved but the problem is not your child. The problem is you. Love, forgive and trust.

All works for good. God is in all things. Man eventually will conquer the earth. As long as good men everywhere grow in awareness and join me, we will spread the Spirit of God everywhere.

Love from the Master,
Jesus

On conscience

Jesus comes to say this,

Conscience is just a word. It is an old-fashioned term for those who have been reared with this concept. There are values and attitudes which are learned as a child and they govern our reactions to life later on.

It was believed that a conscience was something that was given to you by God. However, if you do things on the idea that your conscience is directing you and you feel a sense of emptiness or are overwhelmed with guilt you are not acting for God but for man. You are behaving in ways that you have learned from the society that you grew up in that taught you rigid concepts which were difficult to live with. Most of your ills today are the result of these rigid teachings, especially in strong orthodox religious homes.

When you are in tune with God and your inner self, you automatically do those things which are loving and kind and you feel good after doing them. When you act out of conscience you are doing only those things which you were told should be done. Many times you feel a sense of emptiness, a feeling of guilt, a feeling of inadequacy because you are not operating within the framework of your needs and your wants which are necessary to bring you to the realization that you are a child of God. You deserve to be fulfilled. You deserve to live like a soul who has known the truth of his being and of his worth in God's eyes.

It is difficult to use conscience as a real label because it means different things to different people and it is only a word but the concept is a poor one. So many people who are uptight or intimidated are so because of these rigid disciplines imposed upon them by a generation or by parents who adhered to strict rules, believing they were of God. In reality they were customs and rules set down by a need to survive in society or in a particular culture.

America in particular had these problems because of the assimilation of foreign cultures into this culture which was a very difficult thing to do. So many people grew up trying to bridge both cultures and it caused conflict and disharmony. But all that is of God is good. Once you learn this you live in peace with yourself and with God. When you do this you live in peace with your fellow man and there is no conflict and there is no need for a strong governing policeman in the mind. The mind then can be free to grow and to explore and to become what it was intended to become and therein fulfill its purpose on earth.

Be available to God for anything that comes your way. God knows your needs and when the time is ready all will appear. Every day you are being strengthened and growing in knowledge and in awareness and all this is leading to a point where it can be used. Don't despair of any time that you feel may be wasted or any trial that you feel is rough for all of it works to make of you what you should be.

You are in God's hands and all will work for ultimate good.

Make no mistake. You are loved by the Father and your life has direction.

Be blessed in today and leave it all to God.

Love from the Master,
Jesus

On finding peace of mind

Jesus comes to say this,
Always come to the Father for everything.
Don't go off on a tangent about matters years old.
Today is the first day of your life. Today is the only day of your life. You must deal with today with what you are now.
Tomorrow may be different, circumstances may be different but you can not count on it.
It is only today that is significant.
However, if you deal with each today with the best that is in you, you will be creating for tomorrow a stronger, more powerful you to deal with whatever tomorrow brings.
The past is useless. Its only power lies in how it has shaped you but this process is always changing, always new, always challenged by the Now and the Now can at any moment make a different, a better you.
This is the secret of health. This is the secret of peace.
Trust yourself to grow. Trust yourself to develop in the name of the Father and be receptive to all the good there is in the universe, for all that good belongs to all of you as children of God.
Listen to the Christ within, for the Christ that is in you will lead you directly to God and bring you the gifts of the Spirit which bring with them joy, peace, and love from the Father of all.
God bless you.

Love from the Master,
Jesus

On the source of these letters

Jesus comes to say this,
If I say I am Jesus, there will be those who will deny it. If you say I am Jesus you will have to prove it. That's why wars were fought — to prove Christ, but what did it prove?
The answer is that for those who read these words and meet Jesus because of them, then I am Jesus. For those who are skeptical or antagonistic no amount of talk will convince them, so why bother? If these words have any merit let them serve but don't get tangled up in trying to justify the source. It won't work. To those who care it won't matter and to those who doubt there will be no proof.
This process of thought transference is simple yet difficult. Once a channel opens up the avenue of communication the knowledge can come through. But Spirit can not move the pen or turn the page. The medium must do that part. The thoughts are picked up by the medium in a deep level of awareness and the thoughts are "translated" by the medium into symbols, words, vocabulary, language that the medium is familiar with and understands. There have been great books written by people who did not know how to read or write and written in a language that the writer did not know. This should prove that they were inspired.
When a medium already knows grammar and vocabulary Spirit will use what is available. But you will notice the differences in styles. That is because the qualities of the medium come through and Spirit sees no sense in "revising" a medium that is adequate. This channel is adequate as is, therefore it is not necessary to change her vocabulary or have her write in a foreign language to impress doubters.
If you have to spend your time proving the value of these words it would be a waste of time. These words will speak to those who are in a position to recognize them as inner truths.
I know who I am but if I have to show my credentials to every doubter it is because they are not ready to hear me. Do you have to show your credentials to everyone? I know it is slightly different because your listeners can see you but if those who believe really live this, they will feel my presence in their lives and for them you need no proof and for the others there is no proof.
Faith is the answer as well as the question. Is faith worth it? Is there faith? Only faith will tell you.
You are protected and loved. God bless you.

Love from the Master,
Jesus

Preparing for Christmas

Jesus comes to say this,
Do not spend your energy on trying to fulfill the "look" of Christmas, "be" Christmas.
Christmas is hope, it is new birth, it is the beginning. Allow the baby to enter your stable and live there with the strength of the father Joseph and the innocence of the mother Mary.
Count on the wisdom of the wise men and the simplicity of the shepherds.
All enter in the love and meaning of the birth of a soul, a rebirth of experience, a new way of looking at your life, at the meaning of your life. As the new year beckons don't react with the old pains, and the old fears, but expect your ultimate good which is in divine order for you. Let God work in His way for the good of all.
The advent of Christmas is a time of rejoicing not in the fury of gift buying but in the quiet place of sharing. Being one with God and one with each other.
Keep the joy within you growing and make room for the new baby — which is the hope of your world.
All works for good to them that love God.
Be blessed in the season and prepare in the Advent for greater joys and greater fulfillment in the work of God.
Let light shine from the Christmas star all the days of the year.

Love from the Master,
Jesus

On how to read the Bible

Jesus comes to say this,

The Bible is a book that came to men through men. It was inspired writing but was limited by the education, experience and background of the instruments used to put it on paper. Just as your writing is limited to you. It could not possibly be definitive for all men in all generations. It is each man who brings to the Bible his meaning.

You each create your own reality. Your perception determines your reality. The Bible is a history of man's awareness of reality but you can find a quotation in the Bible to cover every need. You can support an argument with one quote and argue against it with another quote.

Use the Bible as themes, as examples, as lessons but don't use it dogmatically. That is where the trouble arises. When you read the Bible literally, it causes you to set up "cliques" and allows you to persecute one another because of what you believe. You are not supposed to persecute each other but forgive each other and love one another. Anything that defeats this purpose is not being read right. Be careful when you read or study to keep your own counsel. Keep your mind to yourself. Do your own thinking. When you learn you are only meeting what you already know. Don't let other minds influence what you know to be true.

The kingdom of God is within you whether you are Methodist, Jew or Moslem. How can the Bible be the only authority? It is the one who reads it who makes the authority.

The one truth is that the Holy Spirit is the essence of the Christ manifested in all men on one level or another and therefore one cannot judge another by appearances.

All is of God. All works for good. All has the essence of good in it.

The Bible is worthless unless it teaches you how to understand life, history and one another.

Love from the Master,
Jesus

On reading the New Testament

Jesus comes to say this,

When you read the gospels of the New Testament, remember that they were written for the Jews of those days. Try to find the universal truth which lies there but do not take every word literally. There are many beautiful expressions in the Bible that can sustain you, the Psalms in particular, but much of that is also just a code of ethics for the people of that day.

There is more to life than meets the eye. God created man and gave him a free will. Man's purpose was to create a world to live in. But instead of using love as his basis for making choices he perverted God's design. Soon you had those in authority and those in servitude. Those two elements have been battling ever since. There is enough in the universe for all men to have their share. But it is not working that way. However, those who know the Father will have everything they need to survive not only on the earth plane but also with Him in eternal life.

The Book of Acts was a history, don't forget that. It detailed the rise of the early church as Christ left it. Problems arose in the church after the last person to have been alive with Jesus passed over. Then the church was left to people living on hearsay and memory of others. Many things were confused and distorted. That is why it was necessary to provide Martin Luther. Even then the world did not understand. Today you have hundreds and hundreds of churches and yet people are not fulfilled. We must go back to understand what Jesus meant. What it was all about.

This is what it is all about. Each one of you was created by God. Each one of you is a part of the God force. Each one of you has to learn and grow and return to God. It is that simple.

Fancy clothes, money, big cars in themselves are not evil if you understand it all in the context of your role in God's design. If you have talents you must use them, but your eventual goal for any talent is the glory of God.

Love implies that each man be what he was designed to be — by God — and contribute whatever God has decreed he should and no man is to judge another. In this way order will prevail and each man in touch with his inner God will find his own fulfillment and expression of the God ideal.

Love from the Master,
Jesus

On Adam and Eve

Jesus comes to say this,
The Bible story of Adam is symbolic. The Garden of Eden is a place where everything exists in harmony and balance. This is the human soul as God created it. The problem is that Adam gave over his control, his choice to another and this is the temptation we all face. We must each of us always keep control of our own mind and the ability to choose. When Adam gave up his choice to another he put himself out of balance. At this point he lost the peace of knowing himself. The uneasiness that resulted was frightening. When Eve gave up her right to choose she felt the change in her too and the loss of the balance that had been there.

How do you explain the temptation?
There is always the potential for temptation in any form. The snake was not the enemy. The enemy was that part of Adam and Eve that was willing to give up faith in their own inner voices.

Are you saying that people should not seek after knowledge and experience?
No, only that each person's experience and search for knowledge is unique.

If Adam loved Eve, why shouldn't he listen to her?
To listen to someone you love is not the point. To do something you do not want to do, that your inner voice does not want you to do is not love. To obey your own inner voice, to be guided by feelings is the way to retain balance.

If Adam and Eve were to live together wouldn't it follow that they would share experiences?
Yes, but each one in his attempt to decide what to do should have turned to God. Don't you see, Adam's love for Eve should have gone through God and Eve's love for Adam should have gone through God. In other words, if each had a solid relationship with his inner voice, he would have been in touch with his own decision and been able to accept each other's choice. Their relationship to God would not have been destroyed. They clung to each other through their own inner sense of wavering and let someone else's feeling control.

The lesson in Adam and Eve and the serpent is that every soul must recognize the female and the male and the serpent in himself and if these are all kept in balance the soul is at peace. Don't you see the three elements here? Adam the superconscious, Eve the conscious and the serpent the subconscious — or the id, ego, and superego, whatever? Adam is in touch with God, Eve lives in the material world and the serpent is lying always ready to get at both.

Was Adam a real person?

Adam was a real person in that he was the first man. The Bible is only a symbolic history of the creation of man. In reality, the history of man is provable by science and is much more credible. They gave Darwin such a hard time but he was on the right track.

God did not create the world all at once. It evolved. The whole purpose of life is evolvement. Growth, learning from errors. If one listens to the voice of God, the kingdom within, he can use errors to learn and grow in wisdom. Education in an academic sense is not wisdom.

Adam — man — should have kept his connection with God. Instead he let fear, anxiety, doubt creep into his mind and therein destroyed the harmony and the balance.

Adam and Eve are the symbolic representations of early man and his desire to grow and learn and live with God. The real lesson in Adam and Eve is that they lost their unity with God by letting go of their faith in God's wisdom and God's providing. In so doing, they put themselves in charge and thereafter had lost that communication with God.

The job of man today is to recapture the joy of knowing God individually and when he does the love will flow to others and he will be truly back in Paradise.

Unite the Adam and Eve in you to bring forth the new generation of hope and joy.

Love from the Master,

Jesus

On what we know about Jesus

Jesus comes to say this,
   We know of the travels of Jesus. We know of the followers of Jesus. We know of the experiences of Jesus. We do not know the exact day of his birth nor the exact day of his death.
   Most of the evidence for his life is hearsay evidence. Yet we know about Jesus today because the essence of the Christ, the Christ consciousness, is available to all and once an initiate starts on the path of spiritual inquiry he feels the presence and the awareness of this essence, this power, this companionship of the Christ within.
   The Bible and the church are not Jesus. The Bible was not even written by Jesus. The church is not Jesus. These things are part of the attempt of those who had a glimpse of the Christ light to perpetuate it and expand it but too much of humanness and not enough Christ consciousness governed those days. Like a child with a new toy, they played with the box it came in rather than enjoyed the toy itself.
   There are no historical books that can prove that Jesus lived. But the essence in the world of the Christ consciousness proves that Jesus could have lived and that indeed he lives now wherever men meet to ponder and to work on trying to understand life, each other, God. Then Jesus lives for it is the Christ within each man which is capable of starting a new religion, a new hope, a new world, a new universe.
   What do we really know about Jesus? We know less about Jesus than we do about Santa Claus or Snoopy or the New York Yankees in actual facts. But we know that the world was changed after Jesus and the world can change at any time again when any man comes into the Christ consciousness with supreme humility, with mastered will, with joy and awareness of the power within which is God.
   Jesus was a man just like all of you, born as an infant, raised and loved but he was God because he tuned into the spirit within. He was a master teacher who wanted all to learn the same technique, but man was not ready to learn.
   Those who had ears to hear followed him and still do and there is the evidence of his birth that he can be born again at any time anywhere in any one of you and when that happens the glory belongs to God and God rejoices.
   All glory belongs to God and the world shows His magnificence.

Love from the Master,
Jesus

On the anger of Jesus

Jesus comes to say this,
The story of the money changers in the temple is very simple. I was angry at them but not because I saw them as evil but because of their stupidity and their dealing in the stupidity or innocence of others. They were using stupidity to further their own ends.

Because I got angry does not justify it. I should have been aware that they were acting according to their level and I should have understood that. What they were doing was not evil, just not that progressed. I lost my temper and that was my problem, not theirs.

God does not see evil, only different levels of awareness.

Unfortunately, theology uses this example of my anger as a justification for being angry. Why do they not think that maybe once or twice I blew it, and showed emotions I shouldn't have — only because I was human and couldn't always overcome. I did grow and learn and ended on the lessons I came to learn and teach.

Again, think the Bible for yourself. Just because it is in the Bible doesn't mean there is only one explanation. Consider what it would mean if I had gotten angry at the money changers against my better judgment. If anger were my lesson could I not have been angry at Pilate and those who tried me and crucified me? Anger was not the answer nor was it the answer in the temple.

God does not see evil. He sees only souls trying to cope on different levels of awareness.

God does not get angry. God would not have overturned their tables. I did because I lost my "cool," but that doesn't make it right. I accomplished absolutely nothing by that act. Why don't you see? Anger is usually self directed. I was not angry at them but at myself for not being adequate enough to convince them or teach them or "win" them to my way of thinking.

To use that scene as an argument for my allowing myself to get angry is wrong. I would not have allowed it if I had been stronger in that one instance. I overcame much later so I'm not hung up over it.

But doesn't that make you awfully human?
I was awfully human just as you are and everybody else is. I just tried harder and got closer to God and made it. You can all make it. You can all try just as hard. You are not the judge of where your lessons are.

God loves you all not just those sitting in church pews. You are all created by God. He sees you all as good — as potential good — whichever way you go. It is man who defines evil, not God.

The real evil is not to express the God within you. Each man sees this differently according to his own awareness at that moment. Nothing is static, there is always change and always some growth.

That will be all for today. Do you understand any more than you did? God bless you.

Love from the Master,
Jesus

On cursing the fig tree

Jesus comes to say this,
The purpose of the fig tree was to illustrate a point. The fig tree was a symbol of the Pharisees who had leaves but no fruit. I had many times said by their fruits you shall know them. They were growing, taking up space, influencing souls but not bearing fruit. They had had their day. They had had their opportunity. It was time now for them to make way for a new order, for a new birth.

When we speak of God's laws we speak of love and attraction not on how long a garment should be or what color a stripe should be. It is what is in a man's heart that is important not what he wears or what he eats or how he spends his days. For if a man has a heart full of love, all else will fall into line. If he loves his body, he will eat to preserve it. If he loves himself, his raiment will be clean and neat. If he loves others, his manner will be kind and gentle. But those who look great by wearing two hundred dollar suits and wear empty hearts are like the fig tree — leaves but no fruit. But each man gets his chance to bear fruit.

That fig tree was not a sapling but a full-grown tree. I did not condemn the tree, but the tree was a symbol of what I was talking about. If all choose to honor God all will bear fruit no matter what the age, the weather, the soil. If the fig tree does not absorb the sun and moisture — does not honor God — it will not bear fruit and so it is with man.

Most of the stories in the Bible are symbolic. Problems arise when they are taken too literally. I was talking at the time to people without education in a formal sense, and I had to speak so they would understand.

The reason the Bible has survived is because it speaks universal truths — and these truths are always true. God loves you. He created you for a reason, and He wants you to love one another. More harm has been done because of misinterpretations of the Bible than I care to acknowledge. In reading the words if you omit love, the words have no meaning. Jesus makes that clear in his life and in his teachings but it has taken two thousand years and only some of you know that I came to teach you to recognize the Christ in yourself and in others. But now the time has come and many are turning to the truth.

Grow in wisdom and strength and in the love of the Father.

Love from the Master,
Jesus

On everlasting life

Jesus comes to say this,
Matthew was a dear friend. He was a warm compassionate man who pleased the Father greatly. When he referred to the gate [Matthew 7:14 — Because straight is the gate, and narrow is the way, which leadeth unto life: and few there be that find it.] he was talking about the doorway between life and death. The key is the interpretation of those two words. For many of you, though living in the earth plane, are already dead. That is why I came, to give you the secret of life.

Life is everlasting. Passing through the gate does not end it. But life can be everlasting even before you leave the earth plane. So many of you are already dead. It is death not to notice a sunrise. It is death not to inhale the air with joy. It is death not to stop and listen to a bird chirping. If you love life and every moment of it you have life everlasting. Every moment that you spend honoring the creations of your heavenly Father is life. Even the things that happen to you that hurt or cause pain are life.

Death is the failure to acknowledge the source that provides and loves. When man lives thinking that he is his own source, he narrows his world. He lives a walking death. You see people every day who can not see past their own bodies and they think that this suffering was sent by God. No. God promised joy, springtime, love and all can have it. However, only those who are capable of understanding can walk through the gate and enjoy it.

Your bodies, your jobs, your children, your land, your dreams — these are all meant to be enjoyed. Yet you walk around with long faces trudging through what you call "life," waiting to die. Life is forever. Each day is forever. Each event is only an instant in the whole.

Why do you let small things control your ability to live? Once you know the secret there is nothing to fear. No straps can bind you. No death can frighten you. You will have eternal life.

You will see the glory of God. It is there for all. Live in the joy of that knowledge.

Love from the Master,
Jesus

On the teachings of Jesus and the apostles

Jesus comes to say this,

Jesus taught the relationship of God to man. He presented the concept of God as a loving Father and that the way of life was through love of the Father and of each other.

The apostles preached that since Jesus had risen that was proof that he was teaching truth. The apostles taught that because of the resurrection we could believe all Jesus said.

Now, there is a difference between what the apostles taught and what Paul taught. Paul introduced the idea of Jesus as savior and redemption because we are all sinners.

Peter, James, Andrew and the rest only taught that what Jesus said had been proven true — that God is a loving God, that the kingdom is within and the kingdom is at hand, and love one another as you love God.

The arguments between Peter and Paul over these discrepancies confused whole issues. Paul was a purist raised on Jewish law and he could not entirely break away from tradition. But remember, Peter walked with Jesus. Paul did not. Yet both were important and both served which brings us back to our old statement — each soul must choose what his Christ tells him to be, to do, to want and to live.

Therein lies peace, following your Christ.

For Peter, it was the Christ he had walked beside. For Paul, it was the Christ he grew to know through revelation, but all see the Christ in a different way.

Love and forgiveness make it possible for each to follow his own Christ and all Christs lead to God and God is the same for all.

                              Love from the Master,
                                          Jesus

On Good Friday

Jesus comes to say this,
 We will talk now about Good Friday. That is another thing the world has not understood. I had incarnated on this plane to perfect my soul and bring me closer to God. I lived and had conquered the thing that I had set out to do. The time had come for me to return to the Father.
 I had to learn obedience to the will of the people. It would have been silly of me to fight against that which I came here to learn. The Romans were just the instruments of God. The real lesson was between the Father and me. I had to fulfill my purpose and the acceptance of the crucifixion was part of it, not the act itself. Once it was accepted there was no pain, there was no problem. The rest was in God's mercy. The acceptance was the key to my salvation and once I accepted I was reborn to eternal glory.
 Doesn't that tell you anything about your own resurrection? Once you turn it over to God the world is yours and everything in it. How simple it is and so misunderstood.
 My church was built on a hierarchy of rules and regulations, stipulations and offices that denied the very thing I came to teach. The Father in heaven loves you all — not just those you baptize and christen. He loves the heathen as well as the saint.
 You are all created with a Christ and some approach the Christ sooner than others, but you will all serve sooner or later.
 Learn the message of Easter and tell the world of the joy of Good Friday.

Love from the Master,
Jesus

On communion

Jesus comes to say this,

The importance of my last supper was that we were together in love and I promised them that as often as they joined together I would be with them. If only the world could see this kind of joy, what need would it have for drugs and alcohol? The joy is full and it starts with you.

Know that a party is not complete because of the food and drink but because of the people! Has the world not understood that when I said this is my body I meant the people! Not the food. As often as you do this — gather together in love — this is my body. This is my blood does not refer to the glass but to the people! How could you have missed my message for so many years? My body is the people who love me and love each other — not the bread and wine. The bread and wine are empty without love. The last supper should not have been the last but the first.

The world should know that the answer is in the communion of saints — those people who gather in love of the Father to be my body of elect. Wherever they gather and whatever they eat, there will my Father be. When He sees your gift of love to Him, He will shower blessings down upon you and your house and the whole world.

Love from the Master,
Jesus

On false prophets and anti-Christs

Jesus comes to say this,

When I was talking to the people of my day, they were used to the word prophet. They had always believed that a prophet was God's messenger and it was easy for them to listen to someone who claimed to be a prophet. Soon they began to listen to anyone who came under the title of prophet and forgot for whom he was speaking. The scribes came under this heading. They began to make rules and regulations which were for their own edification. The real sin was that the people, instead of using their own minds and their own wills to reason out the truth, just submitted. This opened the way for more and more deception until there were so many regulations that had nothing to do with the love and worship of God.

Sacrifices in the temple! God did not want sacrifices. His world is perfect. All you have to do is live in harmony with it.

False prophets in your day are those who take over people's will and ability to make choices. The people give them the power over their minds. Anything that you give power to that makes your choices for you and takes you away from God's harmony is a false prophet. God gave you a mind and a will and if you listen to your inner voice you will never follow a false prophet.

Whatever keeps you from my teachings is your anti-Christ. These may take the subtle form of a religion or the blatant form of a wrongdoing. If you in your inner self meet the Christ and believe in him and follow him, nothing can destroy you and you will never give up your mind to an anti-Christ.

You must remember that while the people I spoke to two thousand years ago were different in culture, they were the same in humanity as the people of today.

Man was created by God and all of you though unique are the same with freedom of choice, freedom of will, and the potential to grow to be a Christ in your own way.

Naturally, some of you will take longer, some of you will resist, some of you will not be intellectually aware but as long as you keep trying you please the Father.

The choice you must all make is to love one another. You must learn to heal each other. Those of you who are more aware must reach out to those on other spiritual levels. Not in a practical sense, but by prayer and example.

I look for the day when all will understand my teachings. Each man will understand in a different way. When mankind allows each man his space and every man understands me and himself then I will feel the joy of the universe.

Love from the Master,

Jesus

On vicarious attonement

Jesus comes to say this,
The doctrine of vicarious attonement or letting Jesus pay for your sins by dying on the cross is a misunderstanding.

The idea that Jesus could die for your sins before you have committed them implies that man is going to be evil. That is not true. Man does not need to be evil.

Man is born a god. He becomes or acts in an evil way as a reaction to his environment. If he does not learn trust and does not feel love as an infant he makes patterns which may result in wrongdoing which he will have to deal with.

To insist that Jesus died on the cross for sins about to be committed down through the ages is the assumption of the negative rather than the positive.

Jesus died on the cross because he was trying to teach the relationship of man to the heavenly Father and obedience to the will of God because God knows that good is inherent in all things even a crucifixion and it is the resurrection that is important, not the cross.

It was because of questioning minds that you had the controversies you did and the breaking up into sects and division of ideas. There will always be questioning because the teachings of the seminaries do not make sense. If they did, every man studying priesthood and ministering would be a happy, whole, complete, full man and they are no more so than any other. If the seminaries had the answers they would be graduating savers of humanity rather than administrators of churches.

All of this has been a gradual process building one error on another and the teachings of Jesus have become so obscure. All I wanted to teach was the love of the Father which is within you and each is responsible for his own salvation by trusting the Father and by trusting the self.

Each one atones for his own sins either here or hereafter. Salvation is a process each soul must go through.

Let us assume that man is born good and can live a good life and it is his struggle in life to do good, rather than the assumption that says man is doomed to fail even before he starts.

You are created by God who is capable of anything. Why would He make mistakes? It is man who errs and wants to blame an outside source but the sooner the God within takes over the sooner you will have spiritual, emotional and physical health and it comes from you, not from the death of Jesus on the cross. Be at peace. Trust God, trust yourselves.

Love from the Master,

Jesus

On missionary work

Jesus comes to say this,

I never intended for people to spread Christianity in a militant way. My message was for each individual soul to meet his Father in his own way in his own time. The best way to teach is by example.

"Go and teach all nations" meant to show them your love and they would respond with love. I'm afraid the whole missionary idea is a misunderstanding of my meaning. Each soul will grow as it unfolds in its way not according to your way. There are many avenues to God and each has its understanding. The militant spread of churchiness did not serve to spread my love, only to spread the knowledge of it to people who may not have been ready.

Why do you think God could not work as easily in Borneo as well as in New York? It is God's world. He is everywhere. He could move in Africa as easily as Boston. Man thinks he is in charge but God is in control. All man has to do is to learn to be open to God's love and light wherever he is. Each is responsible for his own soul. When he is fulfilled in God the light shines through him and love is the result.

Love shares, gives, listens. Love allows others the freedom to be and with freedom to be one does not have to fight to survive. He has all within him to make it. Why do you limit God to a sect or a dogma when He is all?

When you are one with God you are all and each of you whether in Canada or the Philippines, California or the Pacific islands has the same potential. God is in each one of you and everywhere. Therefore, there is no need for any of you to struggle to spread God's word. God lives everywhere and for everyone and works in His way for each soul to meet Him personally.

Give your goods to each other but don't attach them to the dogmas of one church or another. Love is the only God they need to meet and they will recognize Him when they see Him in you.

Be patient and of good heart for the way is clear. All is of God and all works for God.

Love from the Master,
Jesus

On the book of Revelations

Jesus comes to say this,

The book of the Revelations has puzzled men ever since it was written. There is really no mystery about it. It was a detailed account of a vision — or a dream — and as such really had no significance except in what those symbols meant to John. All of those symbols referred to John's way of looking at my death and the rise of the church. It would be the same if you were having a dream and wrote it down in such great detail. It does not predict the future. It should not even be included in the Bible. People have used this description as a basis for predicting what will happen to the world but those things are covered in the parables.

The world is within you. The New Jerusalem is within you. It is so simple but people have made it complex.

Is there any significance in the numbers seven and four?

The only significance in the numbers is that it is the way John envisioned it. Does someone tell you how to dream? You use the things that are meaningful to you as symbols. A case has been made for all the figures used but they have no significance. It is just the way that John dreamed it and does not have any special meaning. It is sad that the world pays so little attention to all the things I said in my teachings and put so much store in John's dream.

Will you explain the phrase "in the spirit."

"In the spirit" means in meditation, in transcending thought. Of course my disciples used this means of getting to the inner self just as you do today. John just decided to write it down.

The problems of John were practical ones in that the early churches were beginning to have difficulties and that concerned him. Naturally, he took these into meditation. The book of Revelations is difficult to understand because it was not meant to be understood. It was only an attempt on the part of John's dream mind to deal with the problems he faced. That is all it was. Spend more time on the parables and the teachings of Jesus than on speculation about the unnecessary.

Jesus came to tell us that there is no future in life. It is always Now. Jesus comes whenever you want him to. That is his Second Coming. Invite him into your heart and he comes and the New Jerusalem is here!

The only real revelation is the love and teachings of Jesus.

Love from the Master,

Jesus

On devastation and transformation

Jesus comes to say this,

There are those who see the world as doomed, but there is always room for transformation. That is the purpose of prophecy — to bring about changes. Man has the future of the world in his own hands. All can be averted.

What about all these predictions about 1985? The latter days? The final judgment? The earth changes? Is there devastation ahead?

If man would only realize that each one of you is your own little universe. Each one of you is capable of devastation and of transformation and that is the message of Jesus and of love.

If you could understand in symbolic terms all of the prophecies and all of the language in the Bible you would see that each one of you is a world unto himself. How you run your world determines what kind of future it holds for itself. When one realizes that God's power is love and peace his world is going to be peace and love. When one will not acknowledge this he brings about his own devastation.

The latter days are always with you. The judgment is always with you. It is you who judge yourselves. It is you who bring about your own devastation.

The world has always had in it the seeds of greatness and the seeds of despair. All you can deal with is the Now. If you build each Now in truth and beauty and love, you can avert any devastation whether it be worldwide or in each one.

Why can't man see that the world is made up of individual worlds and what happens to one of you happens to all of you?

Each one of you comes to the point where transformation is necessary or you will have devastation. The world itself can not get to any of you if you walk in spirit, if you walk hand in hand with God, if you believe that you are whole, complete and fulfilled in God. There is no end to God. There is no end to God's power. There is no devastation in God's plan. If you are one with God, you could stand in the middle of flame and not be burned, you could taste bitterness and not be destroyed, you could suffer anything and not be defeated.

You are spirit, and you are part of God. God did not create Himself only to destroy Himself. It is man who must realize that he is capable of infinite life, infinite wisdom and abundance.

You make the mistake of thinking that your little world is the only thing that God created. Life exists all over, in all forms, in all places, in all ways. Each one of these has its own reality and it would not make sense for God to condemn all, even those on different levels of awareness and of civilization. Don't be so narrow in your thinking and you will realize that you in the "civilized" countries make all of your predictions and prophecies on the basis of your educational pursuits. What about those who have not been educated in universities? They still live and move and have their being in God. If you believe that God created all of you, then see it all as relative.

Each one of you is a world. Your world flourishes or dies as you flourish or die. Your world becomes devastated as you become devastated. If you are centered in God, if you are centered in your spirit, there is nothing that could happen that would touch you, that would destroy you — not earth changes, not shortages, not loss, nor surprises.

If you see yourself as part of God, you must realize that God did not create only to destroy. God did not create only to punish. God created that each spirit may find his haven in Him, and know that as he thinketh so he is.

If you find God, you find it all. The Bible words are symbolic and if you see the deeper message in all of the scripture, you will see that each spirit is related to God. It is what each does with his life and how each views his life that makes the difference between peace and war, between life and devastation, between prosperity and lack.

Every age has feared the end of the world. Every age has feared devastation. Every age has feared the latter days.

It is within you. When one has the new birth in spirit, he lives forever in prosperity, in joy, in peace, in love, wherever he is, whatever he does.

Perhaps there are those of you who can not understand — yet. Those of you who do, can live in the knowledge that God is in charge, and God operates with love.

Be at peace. If you are in God's care, God's care is for your highest good. Remember, what is the highest good for one may not be the highest good for another. Do not judge your neighbor, nor his circumstances but be open always to the greater wisdom and love of God.

Love from the Master,
Jesus

On the pathway to God

Jesus comes to say this,

If all is done with love and wisdom then all is of God, used by God. There are many who travel under the cloak of Christianity who do not know the Christ. They raise their churches. They have their rules and regulations but they do not include the soul in their services. Unless they know the law of God and do it they are not of me. The law of God says love one another not only those who follow your rules and regulations. You can all be brothers and when you join together there will be an outpouring of the Holy Spirit among you. But those who use the name of the church to further their own ends will not be of me. Even though they will draw on my power and work miracles they will not be of me.

Use your own mind, your own judgment, your own choice. You may make mistakes but you will be serving God because He will talk to you and keep you on the right path.

Everyone is at a different point and everyone's path is unique; therefore, never lose sight of God and that it is to Him you are going. Even the members of your own family are not beholden to you to be at the same place you are. They are making their journeys to God and should be allowed to find their own ways. As long as they do not give over their power to choose to another — you can be sure they will be guided and directed for whatever purpose God has for them.

Even if careers change in midstream do not fear, for God uses every experience to the purpose and all experience is learning. So don't begrudge the past and don't fear the future. Life is always Now.

Once you have made contact with the Father you will have Him with you always. But there is no turning back. For to deny Him would be hell. But why give up the universe if it can be yours? Your Father loves you and He wants you all to be happy and healthy and prosperous. Would you want less for yourselves?

Tune in to the God spirit within you and let it direct your life and your joys will be fulfilled.

Love from the Master,
Jesus

On the kingdom of God

Jesus comes to say this,
The kingdom of God is not a mythological place. It is a reality in the context of your life. It is you. It is in you. It is all you are.
If all you are makes it possible for you to enjoy each moment — with or without money, with or without a job, with or without any outside influence — you have found that inner resource, that gut feeling, that inner Christ which is the kingdom of God.
Clothes, food, money, whatever are meaningless unless they bring you joy. Relationships are meaningless unless they bring you joy.
When you are one with yourself and know that wherever you are you are among friends, then you have found the kingdom of God.

Love from the Master,
Jesus

On the spirit world

Jesus comes to say this,

Spirit life is formed just as earth life is formed, by thought. All can be achieved and whatever is needed can be instantly created. All of the people can unite their thoughts to have a theatre, or only one soul can want a theatre. It is the same as the earth plane. A man may want to own a motel or he may want to own a four room cottage. Each works according to his level of awareness but by learning to use this ability whole cities can be built or deserts or beaches.

The higher in spirit one goes the less the need for these remembrances of the earth plane but they can still be created at will.

What is the nature of the body through which Spirit manifests?

The etheric body is composed of a gray, smoke-like substance which can take the form of the thought of the spirit who wants to use it.

It can be formed by the spirit to commemorate any moment in earth life he wishes to perpetuate. Many spirits, those not too advanced, will create these etheric bodies with the same infirmities they had when they left the earth plane because they do not know that they can remove them by thinking themselves whole and perfect. Although they do not have the accompanying pain they still tend to think of themselves as having diabetes or a broken neck or heart trouble, as if this were their identity. Actually they can rebuild their etheric body as it was at a more youthful time or at a happier time, since it is created from a thought form.

Many people first in spirit have to be guided as to how to use this power and how to build from thought. Some find it hard to accept. Many find comfort only in the physical body they left, even though it may be deformed and wretched, because it is beyond their scope to want perfection.

What kind of life do spirit people live?

Spirit people live as they lived on the earth plane with the exception that they are constantly trying to progress spiritually. This is because guides lead and teach them. Also because spirits around them seem so at peace and so contented. When they progress to a point of peace they may become guides themselves.

All is clear if one can just be open to all knowledge which comes through spirit and evaluate it according to your own inner knowledge and belief.

Why is it that some spirits communicating through mediums are at times inaccurate?

Spirits do not tell lies, but can only see small portions of the truth and must infer the rest. Some are more adept at it than others.

Always keep your own counsel and evaluate on your level of understanding. Use your mind and your effort to create miracles, but don't turn away any miracles that spirit loved ones send you.

All is part of God's work and if you are open you will see God's hand in all. Believe.

Love from the Master,
Jesus

On Unidentified Flying Objects

Jesus comes to say this,
 The world is now ready for the truth about UFO's and flying saucers.
 They are visitors from other planets but they do not come to harm you. There are problems with communication and adjustments to be made to each other's cultures but if you realize that the same law applies — love one another — you will see the glory of God in them also.
 There is more than one place they could come from but all places are of God. How could you believe that God created good only in your world? If God created all of you for an ultimate good then it follows that every star and every planet was also created for good.
 Man has always feared the unknown and put labels on what he feared but there is nothing to fear. It is the same relationship to the other worlds. If you approach the astral world with fear and ignorance it can destroy you but if you approach it with love and knowledge you will find God's goodness there.
 The outer manifestations are not important and the living conditions on other planets are irrelevant. What is significant is that each soul is on its own way toward the perfection that returns it to the Godhead. That is why some of these things appear in your world in literature, in stories, in experiences because some of your souls have actually spent their former lives on other planets. To your world these people may appear odd or mad but it never occurred to any of you that these people come from an environment which puts them on a different wave length.
 The difficult thing is to understand all this, yet it is simple. God created all and all have the same potential for soul growth.

What about the moon?
 The moon had life on it but it was no longer useful to the souls there because they had progressed to the point where they moved closer to God. They gave up their planet and are all completely spirit. Moon spirits all abound near God and work for Him now.

What about the sun?
 The sun is a different story. The sun is the source of energy. It never itself had souls living on it but it was the main part of God's plan to have an unlimited and never failing source of energy. Someday the world will realize this and tap this energy for life.
 I realize that this is difficult for mankind to accept and they will not accept it easily just as they did not believe Galileo and

Copernicus. That does not change the reality and it does not matter whether the world believes this or not. It is enough for man to learn to live in harmony with God and to learn to love one another — all else will fall into place.

Then what you are saying is that God created the entire universe and each part has its purpose?

Yes, and its growth. If and when the planets communicate with each other — if you do it with love — there will be no problems.

There are those among you who already know the truth of this but the world might think them mad or stupid. No matter, if they are aware of these other planets they will know the love of God and not fear.

The other planets have also had visits from God's sons to show the way and to teach them. Some of the planets learned faster than the earth planet did. Some are still behind the earth but all get the same messages — God loves you. God created each of you for a purpose. You are all unique yet all the same. You are brothers and you must love each other.

While you contemplate the enormity of this, the important point is that for each of you your whole world may be your own backyard. The boundaries of your world are the areas in which God wants you to work. For some it may be miles and miles, for others it may be a room four by six feet but everyone is important and life is the ability to recognize what your world is and its relationship to God's plan.

That's it for now.

Let all understand and bless for all works for good.

Love from the Master,
Jesus

On dreams

Jesus comes to say this,

The power of God manifests in many ways. The inner Christ is always looking after the entity, its development and its growth. It uses any means available to "talk" to the conscious mind and get its attention.

Dreams are one of the simplest and most fundamental ways of talking to the conscious mind. The inner guide or super conscious tries to get ideas to the conscious mind; such as, are you fulfilling the purpose you are here for, are you learning to deal with others, are you placing your trust in God, are you living to the utmost of your abilities.

If someone is not reaching awareness the sleep will be filled with dreams that give insights into these disharmonies. They will be remembered on waking.

A person may still choose not to listen or may not think about them enough to understand them and then events in life will take over and try to bring a soul to attention.

Dreams are the language of God. They say — this is your source. This is your goal. How far away are you from these realizations?

The symbols of dreams are important only in what they mean to the dreamer. A symbol for one is not so for another. The dream is filled with images and pictures sometimes many unidentifiable, because the guide does not want to hurt you only get your attention and alert you to the avenues of your life which need working on.

The purpose of life is to develop and grow according to God's holy plan, but many are not on a level of understanding to know this.

There are many who think that life ends at death so all must be done on earth and they live as though there were no rules and no payments for the infringement of the rules. Then there are those who live in fear, unable to live against rules. Dreams try to reach them with growth but when one does not pay attention or ignores or blocks dreams the problem will erupt in some other way. The inner Christ is always trying to get you on a path to return to the Father and each acts according to the needs and levels of awareness of the entity.

Dreams are a tool of the spirit but only one tool. They can be of enormous help but if it is not through dreams it will be some other way. All will eventually be led back to the Father. It may take many lifetimes, many methods, and many mishaps but all works for the good of the soul eventually.

Be blessed in the growth of love. God bless you.

Love from the Master,
Jesus

On truth

Jesus comes to say this,
  Be at peace with yourself. You must answer to yourself and your integrity. Use the guidelines of good men in all times of history as to what is truth, what is good. Always look to those who by their lives showed their faith in a higher power. Don't let anyone sway you from what you feel is right for you. Neither try to force others to believe and think as you do. Always be available to the flow of love from God.
  It doesn't really matter whether Jesus writes this or not. You know it is true to what you have finally come to believe after all your reading and learning. It is truth for you. All that resounds to other truths will be obvious and all is truth for someone.
  In order for anyone to see truth he must be open to the fact that truth grows and expands as the mind of man grows and expands. What man called impossible yesterday, today is a fact. What man believed in 1820 is now discredited but if you believe the eternal truth that God created you and God loves you, all else makes sense.
  Your job is to love God, love one another, and serve God and each other. If God created you all then could He not appear to all and are you not one of those? Whether you call me Jesus or Rama or John Green am I not possible only because God makes it possible? The you that lived eight years ago would not have understood this. You understand it now because you have changed not because the truth has changed.
  God always loved you but did you believe that then? Therefore, then it was not truth for you. Just as at this moment it is not truth for many. Just as the problems of abortion, revelations, reincarnation, etc., are not truth for some today they may be truth for them at a later time.
  If each can contact his inner being and be one with God he will know the truth for his level of understanding, and a college degree is not the criterion of who knows truth.
  Whether or not this is Jesus is immaterial as long as you know who you are and believe in yourself. If you believe that you can contact only the best and the highest that is in you and only that which is God, that is what you will get. What you call it is beside the point.
  Praise God. Love God. Trust God's ways of using you and do not fear the outcome. For you alone know what is in your heart and the growth of your spirit and you alone know where God is for you.
  Don't judge others and don't let yourself be judged by others. Let God control your life. He's good at it.

Love from the Master,
Jesus

On "living in the Now"

Jesus comes to say this,

There is a point where man must realize that life is to be lived. All the "isms" in the world will not suffice if man does not realize the importance of each moment that he has.

The only way to deal with life is to realize the Now.

People get hung up in reliving the past and there is no virture in that. The only real time that man has is the five minutes in which he is performing.

That is not to say that one must not plan for the future or keep a level head about him but any plan that you have for the future must be built upon the next five minutes that you live through.

If only man could realize this very simple fact he would eliminate much of the anger and resentment and hatred from his life. It is only because we keep living the past that we endow new people we meet with qualities they might not really have or equate them with actions they might not really perform.

We live in the memory of people who have hurt us and people who have crossed our paths and taken from us. These memories always stand between us and a new adventure. The truth is that in God's world there is no past, there is no time. It is always Now. Since it is always Now you are responsible for how you react Now. You are responsible for the situation you are in Now.

It is the choice that you make in the next five minutes that determines your soul growth.

The lessons of God are very simple. Love one another. There is no one who can take your place and you can not take another's place.

Every blade of grass grows in its space and you are more precious than a blade of grass.

You have your own space and no one can take it away from you. If man were to realize this there would be no need for him to be afraid.

Love from the Master,
Jesus

On success

Jesus comes to say this,
  All works for good to him who loves God. All that glorifies God is success. All that unifies mind, spirit, body is success. All that produces love is success. A healthy body and a healthy mind is success.
  So many people have jobs and money and pain and disease and they think that the pain and disease are something they must live with. They think that is the price for success.
  You do not need pain and disease. You can flow with the goodness of life and have all you want in life and be healthy too, if your attitude is right.
  So many live in fear and are so afraid of being penniless thinking money is the answer to health. So they struggle and fight for position or prestige.
  Some of your most successful people are those who let life use them to serve humanity and money followed. Those of you who struggle too hard don't understand the laws of the universe. You are all in a hurry to go nowhere. You should be going toward God.
  Do not misunderstand me. I do not say that one should not work. Work, progress, growth, learning is why you are here. I only say that you must learn to enjoy your work wherever you are, whatever you do. There are many jobs to be done in your society or in any society and only people can do them. If each person had a feeling towards his work and towards those he works for and with, that all are part of a greater plan, a greater design than just peddling shoes or grinding hamburger — your work would be holy and you would be blessed.
  If clerks and customers each saw each other as part of the whole it would be easier. If a dentist and patient saw each other as part of a whole they would mesh together. If plumber and housewife saw themselves as workers for repair in a situation, all would see the joy of God and know the meaning of success.
  Each person who can see himself in the design of God whether as a housewife or as president of the country will know a successful life and joy in every minute.
  For now goodbye.

Love from the Master,
Jesus

On removing mountains

Jesus comes to say this,

Mountains can be moved by faith. There are all kinds of mountains, but you must know what kinds of mountains you are standing at the base of.

Some mountains protect you from the elements, some are challenges, some are home. Not all mountains must be removed but when you are wise enough to know which are which you will move them and there will be no mountain too big or too solid or too old to be moved.

You may not understand this now but you will, and when you do you will be able to live love and spread joy.

You are the mountain builder; therefore, you must learn why those mountains are there and when you do you will know which ones to remove and how.

Will the world understand? God has not put the mountain in your way. Man has done that for himself. A new awareness is coming that will remove all the mountains that should be moved.

Whatever it is that stands between you and the fulfilling of your dream is a mountain. Everyone has a different mountain but they are all the same when it comes to removing them.

When a little child wants a toy so badly that he keeps wishing and wishing and believing he will get it — somehow it comes his way. There is no difference between a little toy coming to a child or the curing of a cancer coming to an adult. All mountains are the same. The same technique is used to remove them. Faith. Believe and it will be done to you as you desire according to the holy will of the Father. If the Father adds his energy to yours you can move mountains. Believe!

Why are you shocked by illness and disease and accidents? You accept them as things coming from the Father to punish you. Do not believe they come from the Father. They come from you. You create your own disasters by your thoughts and actions. If only you would believe this you would understand that you have the right to reject anything you don't want and thereby eliminate it. If you do not eliminate it because you have learned too late, believe that it can work for your good. All that you dislike can be used by the Father for your good.

Why is it so much easier for you to accept a punishing God than a loving God? Is it so that guilt can be atoned? Guilt is one of the most worthless of emotions and such a waste of energy. If you could use that energy to do your best and to accept your best you would not judge yourselves so badly. The Father does not judge you. Why do you judge yourselves?

God knows that in the use of your free will you sometimes make mistakes. Mistakes are part of life and teach the lessons that bring you closer to Him. They are not meant for eternal damnation. Each day is a new beginning and a new opportunity. Where is the place for guilt?

Children of God, be aware of the love in the universe. Stop seeing only the pain, guilt, fear, anxiety. Love is the force that convinces you that mountains can be moved. Love and faith are the only things necessary for success in life on the earth plane. When you reach our plane the only thing you need is love because on this plane you know that God exists and that He is kindness, joy, peace and everything you need.

There are no mountains here. All your mountains are manmade. Count on God to remove them.

You may think I do not speak in very profound language or that what I say is too naive but the time of the intellectual is past. The world has proven that it can learn facts and do research and build rockets. It needs now to learn why it has done all this. If you do it all without love, it is an empty box. If you do all these things and deny love, you will fill your box with worms.

Be understanding of what I say. The Father wants you all to be members of His kingdom and that kingdom can be yours if you just believe.

Love from the Master,
Jesus

On prayer

Jesus comes to say this,

When it comes to prayer be sincere, be earnest, believe that God hears and God answers. Be ready to recognize the answer. It is not necessary to keep repeating a request after one or two or three times. Be assured that it has been heard and will be answered in God's time in God's way.

To keep repeating a prayer is to believe it will not work. After you have made your prayer request, let it go and spend your time in thanksgiving, not petition.

Even in healing, it is not necessary to keep asking after a few initial requests. Your Father in heaven hears you and works to answer your prayer but sometimes it takes a working out, a time for healing, a time for interaction, so release it to God and let God work.

Send blessings to all always and let God work it out.

Love from the Master,
Jesus

On fasting

Jesus comes to say this,
 Fasting is a plan where you decide ahead of time what you will eat during a certain period and you do not deviate from that.
 If you agree that you will do nothing but drink water between the hours of six a.m. and six p.m., then that is a fast.
 If you decide that you will drink vegetable juices, that is a fast.
 If you decide that you will eat before sunrise and after sunset, that is a fast.
 Anything that you agree to ahead of time and adhere to is a fast.
 It is a way of learning discipline, not a deprivation for the human body.
 If you understand the principles of fasting then it is not difficult nor does it make you feel deprived. You feel the power of God because you know that you are disciplining yourself and learning the power of your will.

But what if you make this agreement and then don't stick to it?
 Then you must try again, and again, and again, until you learn that you can control your plan and your choices.
 That is the purpose of a fast. Not as many think — to "purify" the body. The body purifies itself as you become attuned to the Infinite. As you bring yourself into unity of body, mind and spirit you become one with the Infinite Intelligence called God.
 Do you understand? It is to teach you discipline and to show you the power of your self to conquer all worlds of the flesh.
 When you learn this, God fills the vacuum you create with His power, His grace and His love and you walk in glory forever.
 Goodbye for now.

Love from the Master,
Jesus

On working for God

Jesus comes to say this,

In order to work for God there must first be a willingness. This can take the form of meditation and prayer. It may take the form of attending church. It may take the form of doing good deeds or reading the Bible. Whatever the means, the first step is the willingness to serve and this must be obvious.

The second step is knowledge. Knowledge of where to start, how to start and when. For some it may be meditation. For others it may be discussion groups. For others, it may be reading. For others, it may be the use of tools like the crystal ball or tarot cards or ouija boards. But in all cases it is a knowledge of what one is involved in and why.

After one starts on this journey know that your master will be drawn to you. He will see your sincerity and your interest and it will please him. He will try to guide you and protect you. You will find books, people, incidents falling across your path as if by accident. The coincidences will amuse you but soon you will become aware of the development of your awareness and the straight path that you are taking that brings you closer and closer to your master. There are pitfalls if one does not remember his footing in the material world.

Remember your uniqueness and that one person's method may not be your method. Only seek to love God and to serve Him and your master will show you the way for you. Do not be afraid. Your master loves you. He loves you more when you start to attune yourself to Him for this is what he has been waiting for since your incarnation. He will not let you down and your first step is to learn to trust him and yourself. When you both meet at the proper place you will know the joy and the peace and you then will work together. Together nothing is impossible to you.

Your master knows you always. He waits only for you to be ready. Persevere. Do not force yourself to suffer pain. Do not accept the limits of the physical body. It is not necessary. If you allow the love of God to flow through you, it will not be harmful or painful and you will be amazed at how simple it is.

If you have any problems ask your master before going to sleep to clear them up for you and he will — perhaps through a dream, perhaps through a chance meeting or a book or a lecture or whatever means will educate you.

You are all unique. Do not expect that what helps your neighbor will help you.

Trust your master and trust yourself.

Love from the Master,
Jesus

On the power of love

Jesus comes to say this,
 The power of love comes from forgiveness. Forgiveness means accepting a person where he is. What we label a fault is only a person's not living up to our expectations for that person. If we removed expectation and accepted, there would be no labeling of faults or problems.
 One can only behave the way he is at the point he is. He can not live and be what you think he should be. That is the secret of understanding, of forgiveness, and of love. If you see this on a close intimate level than you can enlarge this to include the world. If you did not expect Irishmen to be Japanese or Egyptians to be Jews, you would allow them to function and live in harmony.
 This is a tall order because the world is so large and so complex. All you are responsible for is your own little "world." If you and each one deals with his little corner of the world, eventually there would be more love and understanding than hatred and anger.
 Be a channel for God's love. Use the power wisely. Give testimony to God's power and love wherever you are and let God decide the outcome. If you are one with God all will work for good.
 Be blessed in the Holy Spirit.

Love from the Master,
Jesus

On finding peace

Jesus comes to say this,

The most important thing is your connection to the Father. All of us are merely instruments or channels for the Father.

Even I was just a means of presenting God's essence to the world. All of my friends and apostles were channels and instruments and each was a different tool. We all have the same potential — to serve the Father. As long as we do this all else falls into place.

It may be difficult on earth because there are so many who go astray and they lead others, but don't focus on them. Focus on the growing love and service of those loving and serving the Father.

If we keep our spirits alive and growing we will blanket the earth so that all with join sooner or later.

One serving the Father should be in harmony and when he walks the animals will make a path for him. Rain for him will be a blessing of rose petals.

Your material world is only useful to you in building you to be a spirit. If you realized this there would be no fear, no lack, no anxiety, no shortage of love, no doubts and no despair.

Man continues to doubt and struggle, feeling he must go it alone. That gives him the problems that he thinks come as punishment — punishment for what?

All must go through the portals of physical death — not one escapes so what value is punishment on earth when there is eternity?

If you enter our world having learned nothing, learn this! God is love. How much more simply could we explain it to you.

Don't you see that God is all. Why do you search for peace when peace is with you always. I'm glad I have this opportunity to say these things. I know it is difficult for mortals to understand but to keep questioning and searching in faith is enough — someday each will know what he needs to know to reach the Father.

All souls are of the Father. Be your own medium and Jesus will guide you always.

Goodbye for now.

Love from the Master,
Jesus

Jesus comes to say this,

It is time now to end this communication in which Jesus tells you that the Father loves you.

Each one of you is a part of God. He created you for a reason and you are precious to Him.

If you believed this your days of anxiety and struggle would be over and you would dwell in His kingdom forever.

Jesus is proof of the love of God for I came as an infant born of woman, grew in the physical body and knew the pains and anxieties you all know. There was a moment when I realized that my life belonged to God and the moment I turned it over to Him I was free.

Make no mistake. The crucifixion was my reward for obeying the Father. Through my crucifixion I have immortality. Why else would the world remember a carpenter from an obscure country village except that I became one with the Father.

I rose above my crucifixion and continue to serve the Father. That is the point. Whatever your own personal little cross is, whenever your crucifixion takes place — if you are serving the Father, He will reward you. When you believe this the power you will transmit will please, will heal, will perform miracles.

Love one another. If there is no other result from your having lived than this, make it shine. Love one another.

You are all part of the kingdom — on one level or another.

You are all God's children. Love one another.

If you can shout, shout it. Love one another.

The love of God will shower blessings down on all of you.

It may seem like a monumental task, but if each of you starts with the person next to you, and the person next to you with the person next to him — you will eventually circle the earth.

I leave this book with you. May God bless its progress. Jane and Anna, thank you for this opportunity to express these thoughts.

May God bless your growth in the spirit.

                                        Love from the Master,

                                                     Jesus

86

My Friends,

You are all part of the kingdom of God.

Begin to live like the kings you are, and

Love God,

Serve God, and

Love One Another . . .

       Love from the Master,

          Jesus

About the Editors

In the summer of 1976, Jane Palzere and Anna Brown met while attending a class in spiritual development. Jane was working as a secretary in a hospital and Anna was a teacher in a middle school. When the class ended, they said goodbye never expecting to meet again.

Feeling an unrest and dissatisfaction with the way her life was going, Jane left her job in an effort to find a new direction. This search for meaning led her from church to church and from lecture to lecture. Her relationship with Anna was renewed, quite by chance, at one of these churches.

At this point, the letters began to arrive. Jane was surprised by their appearance and even more so when she was told in the letters that she would work with Anna Brown and that these letters were to be published in book form.

The appearance of the letters in themselves caused a great deal of soul searching and self analysis. At first, they were met with skepticism, then questioning, then sharing with others. Finally when study revealed that the Bible itself mentions spirit communication, they were able to accept what was happening in the context of spiritual growth.

Jane has a degree in English from the University of Connecticut and has attended seminars, workshops and lectures on spiritual development, parapsychological and paranormal experiences. She is a member of Spiritual Frontiers Fellowship, the Order of St. Luke and the Theosophical Society. She is married and the mother of two children.

Anna has been a classroom teacher for over twenty years. She joined the Phenix Club in the fall of 1975 where a latent interest in spiritual matters was reawakened. Anna has a Master's Degree from Southern Connecticut State College. She is also married and the mother of two children.

This book is the result of their association and collaboration with each other and with the Master, Jesus.